WHEN SECRETS COME TO LIFE

THE HAUNTINGS OF EVERYDAY PEOPLE IN CONNECTICUT

DONNA KENT

AMERICA
THROUGH
TIME

America Through Time
Fonthill Media LLC
www.through-time.com

First published 2025
Copyright © Donna Kent 2025

ISBN 978-1-63499-507-8

All rights reserved. No part of this publication may be reproduced, stored in a retrieval system or transmitted in any form or by any means, electronic, mechanical, photocopying, recording or otherwise, without prior permission in writing from Fonthill Media Inc.

Typeset in 10pt on13pt Sabon
Printed and bound in England

FOREWORD

Let me tell you about my mom. She's like a lot of moms; she baked cookies, drove my sister and I to school back in the day, and, of course, took embarrassing baby pictures of me—with orbs and mists in them. Thankfully, she hasn't shared all of them with the internet, or in this book!

Okay, maybe she's not like your mom, unless they were on *Sightings* and *Ghosthunters* and TV shows like that. Maybe your mother has been interviewed by *The New York Times* and *The Wall Street Journal*—for ghost hunting? If so, well then you can relate.

She's semi-out of the business now but decided to look back and tell some of the stories that still sometimes keep her up at night. When my mom brought to my attention that she wanted me to write the foreword to her third book on ghost hunting, I won't deny I was rather surprised. Her books have always had personal touches diving into the random side quests that she has to partake in, in order to get a certain shot or experience. But never as direct as this. I feel with this book, she really tells the full story of how she began ghost hunting, and the toll that dealing with the spirit world, almost always at the behest of others, has on a person's life. Think *Death of a Salesman* but with a paranormal angle. No stone is left unturned with this book as she bares her soul and shortcomings and how she learned to overcome them in order to succeed and do her very best in this ever-expanding field of exploration. There are a few exclusives that have never been told by any other ghost hunter, but in this book, from her own point of view, she speaks of things that other investigators don't dare mention.

Though I myself am not involved with the work of the paranormal, I am all too familiar with it. I lived it. I witnessed so many things daily that simply had no natural explanation. She always believed me, unlike other parents who are quick to dismiss a child's experiences as fantasy or imagination; she knew it was neither. And then she fixed it. I cannot recall ever being bothered for long by any spirit once she heard about it.

I'm glad she kept a pretty concise record of the events that happened in my childhood home because I've pushed a lot of it out of my mind or it is now just a blurry memory. I do remember certain things from that era involving the paranormal that I will never forget.

One particular night still sticks out; it involved "the girl with the scribbly hair" who appeared before me in my room. I retold this for *World's Scariest Ghosts: Caught on*

When Secrets Come to Life

Tape in the late '90s to coincide with the release of the movie *The Sixth Sense*. I still remember her fairly clearly. I remember the film crew coming to our house for an entire weekend from California—a weekend when I had the flu, and unlike everyone else, was not really interested in being on camera. The highlight of that, as a six-year-old, was the producers playing "rock-paper-scissors" with me (letting me win most of the time) for real dollars. I remember quickly converting that into comic books the first chance I got.

I'm glad she touches on the unglamorous side of working with (some, not all!) film producers as so many investigators are unaware of the reality of how it all goes down. It really is not all that it's cracked up to be or that even a national show will make you famous overnight. Not that she regrets doing the shows or the newspaper and magazine interviews, but she lets the reader know it's probably not how you would imagine it to be and worse, the end result of which you have no editing control, can paint you to look anyway they please once you've signed the release form. I know that for all the shows she's done over the years, the only one who made any monetary payment was the ABC special I mentioned above. Probably because I was in it (just kidding Mom!).

My mother taught me that while the history of a location can be paramount to figuring out details of a haunting, the lifestyle, certain decisions, and actions of the people being affected are just as important. This is especially true when trying to clear the space or the people who are having those problems in the first place. Unlike her first two published books for History Press, now Arcadia (she's written others, but they are self-published), in which she had to focus primarily on a property's history, and less on the ghosts, this time my mother really gets to delve more into the actual events that happened with photographic evidence to match. To this day, some of these (award-winning) pictures are hailed as the best documented and most genuine out there.

Her ability to demonstrate her craftsmanship when it comes to the retelling of certain events has greatly improved over the years, although she still writes just as if she's talking to you face to face over a beer or a cup of coffee and that has been her signature style all along and what brings her readers back for more. She is very relatable and people from all over the world write and email their experiences to her.

I understand she has plans to write about more of her adventures in this field from her cases in other states and even other countries she's visited. "There is no lack of the spirit world, it's all around us," she has said, and I'm sure she'll include the photographic proof of it, as well.

Justin Quinn

PREFACE

You're going to notice that the stories take place more than twenty years ago. Not to worry, age has not dimmed the impact of these tales. You'll also discover it's very different from my previous books that focused on historic Connecticut locations and not so much on average everyday people's houses or occurrences. This book reveals more of the dirty, low-down, nitty-gritty aspects of spiritual infestations in real life than the faded stories of history's ghosts and past.

I no longer investigate, do tours or classes, or really deal with the paranormal unless there is an emergency situation where I can be of help to someone—I do not go looking for it. Nor is it for lack of interest; this book is clearly an indication of that. It's the little things that hunting ghosts will do to you; like drain your wallet, consume massive amounts of your time and energy, make people do and say the most ridiculous things when you're risking your neck to help them, and the fact that the entities can and will come back to get even with you, for daring to attempt to break their stronghold over these people and places.

There is the whole issue of getting rid of the stuff once you find it. There are very few—and I mean very few—people who actually have the knowledge and ability to take on these entities bothering the client and clear them out. Next, you must then have the fortitude and ability it takes to bear the brunt of those creatures' wrath for nearly a decade. I was so very blessed to have the mentors, guardian angels, and the higher power of God watching over me that it's almost unbelievable, considering all the situations I've been in to come out the other side relatively unscathed.

There is a little-known factoid that is left out of every book on how to clear houses and/or people of ghosts, creatures that have never lived, etc., they can come back every three years for a total of nine to bother you and the people you've helped. How can these beings do that? How can they target decent families and people who aren't seeking them out? How are folks who don't even believe in a spirit world becoming afflicted? Because it's allowed. Because in the end, it proves the existence of God. Think of it as a test to see how sincerely the investigator is committed to helping people and whether those reasons are just out of one's ego or pursuit of monetary gain. It is a surefire way to make a non-believer into one.

I found with the investigations that some clients are not willing to put in the same time or effort to help themselves that I put forth on their behalf. Heck, they'd lie right to my face about all kinds of things that helped get them into the mess they were in. They'd deny any involvement with the occult (until I'd unearth a Ouija board hidden in the attic or the stacks of spell crafting books shoved under the bed) or the medications they'd taken (legal or otherwise) etc. They were often averse to or disregarded the sound moral advice offered to them (start with these prayers daily or come clean about your affair to your spouse or stop doing this or change that). They wanted a magic pill or spell to fix their situation instead of the hard work it takes to go about changing their lifestyle and bad habits that drew the negative energy to them in the first place. If a case was over my head and the occupants couldn't or wouldn't follow the simplest of tasks for their own benefit, I'd call in or turn the case over to mentors with my assessments. Conversely, for the homeowners who understood what was at stake and what they needed to do to make a change, it was an honor to be of assistance.

Secondly, as for teammates, my best piece of advice is to choose them wisely. It's so hard in this field because not only do people often represent themselves as what or who they aren't, but that the spirits can and do influence people. It's tricky to say the least. I've always said that your group of investigators should have a relationship akin to police officers and their partners—they all know each other, respect each other, and most would literally risk their lives for one another. At the very least you have to know they've got your back. You have to know their characters, quirks, and personalities so that if or when they start acting unlike themselves, you know what to do! And *vice versa*!

I've worked with many remarkable people who all lent their own special insight and knowledge to the investigations. Everyone has their own talents; in fact, I was never any good at capturing EVPs, for me it was always the photographs. Others were great at writing up their reports of the case or had technical experience in running audio or video equipment. We were by no means perfect, but somehow, we always made it work. There were, however, a handful of people over the years I really had no business working with; there are too many reasons why to list, but for the most part, they just didn't take it as seriously as I felt they should have. Some had entirely the wrong motivations which were contradictory to my own and some were just downright psychopaths. Did I mention that this field is a magnet for kooky people? Be warned! It might sound funny in writing, but I'm not joking! I learned the hard way. Allowing or accompanying these folks on significant investigations was a mistake on my part; I often ignored red flags and broke my own rules to accommodate others. I tried giving people a chance, knowing we all have to start somewhere, just like I did, as you'll see in the chapters that follow. But this field is not for everyone, and people's lives can be ruined or made worse by the grifters and charlatans that gravitate towards those who are vulnerable and afraid. There were people who infiltrated the society to try and enhance their own group (instead of just asking for my advice or help), some who used my good name and connections to weasel their way into locations I'd established a rapport with and even my photoshoots and interviews! I learned what a "coattail-rider" is! I could write a book on things not to do—I can see it now: *The Book of Blunders, Bloopers and Banshees!*

Running a monthly meeting, classes, or slide presentations for over two decades straight was nothing short of miraculous, and I had many great times, discussions,

Halloween parties, and camaraderie with paranormal enthusiasts of all degrees. But it took a lot of really hard work and coordination to keep it going, and that, I don't miss at all!

COVID-19 pretty much killed the tours, which was in its own way very convenient for me because it was around that time that I was conflicted about promoting ghost hunting as a fun, lighthearted endeavor for the tourists and the truth of knowing the seriousness of the subject matter. I had plenty of adventures with the guests (many from out of state), the owners, and hosts of the sites we'd visit. Not to mention all the great food and the complimentary lodgings they would provide to me and, frequently, members of Cosmic Society. Being the director of the tours, I researched all the places we'd visit, making sure they were truly haunted and worthy of inclusion. In these settings, it was easy and enjoyable. What was concerning were the times that sensitive people would be adversely affected at the haunted locations—many times they became overwhelmed, and I'd have to step away from my role as tour guide (and the other guests) and minister to them. Many skeptics changed their views on the supernatural after a Haunted CT Tour; in fact, they were often prime targets for an encounter of some sort.

If you haven't noticed, the encouragement from TV and the internet to become involved with other-worldly pursuits is more prevalent than it ever was before. Fortune telling, dabbling with Ouija boards, tarot cards, and other divination tools are promoted as self-help techniques and are downplayed on purpose. It's like a gateway drug that seems innocent and fun at first, until it's not, until it's too late. I know from firsthand experience as a former tarot card reader.

Recently, the Vatican held a press conference saying that they "are very interested in supernatural phenomena, aliens and apparitions." By the way, this is the first press conference on this topic, UFOs, and mysteries by them since 1978. So why now? It was years ago that they claimed their Vatican observatory telescope, named LUCIFER (Large Binocular Telescope Near-infrared Spectroscopic Utility with Camera and Integral Field Unit for Extragalactic Research), could detect the spirit realm. So why is the Vatican suddenly so prescient?

We are at a time in history where the unseen is becoming unmasked (as the Bible predicted in Luke 21:26) and that "Men's hearts shall fail them for fear, and for looking after those things which shall come upon the earth." I feel like we're at this point and that "those things" aren't coming, they're already here.

Recently it was announced on national television that a new syndrome called "prosopometamorphopsia" was discovered, wherein people had a "disorder" that their brains would interpret a human face transforming into demonic-looking ones. Could it be a way to hide what is really happening in the world? That more and more people are actually witnessing people transforming? Shapeshifting? How devious to blame it on the people who can see than to admit that the time has come that what walks among us will no longer be able to disguise their true identities. There was a time when it was just our cameras picking up entities and beings that we couldn't necessarily see with our own eyes, but yet was there right beside us all the whole time, as this book will prove.

OK, now let's get back to why you haven't heard from me in awhile. And I really hate to say this, it's the whole age thing. Life gets in the way. Things change; you get divorced, the kids go to college, you change careers, whatever. Time catches up with us all, and the old goals and endeavors I had, I've accomplished. My interests, outlooks, and areas of research are a combination of what's new and exciting to me now. Studies or hobbies that had been on a back burner, I can now start thinking about.

So, even though I'm no longer pursuing the paranormal, I'm by no means done with it or the spiritual aspects of the world around us. Once you learn it's actually a tangible thing, your outlook on life and death are forever changed. Not to mention I have volumes of stories, cases, and places from the past (the 2000s were even weirder than the '90s!) to write about in the future.

I do want to thank those who took part in Cosmic Society over the years and your contributions in any way, shape, or form—foremost your honest efforts—for which I am grateful. And to the clients who invited us into their homes and lives in a time of need. To those who have graced us with your time, your experiences, your trust, and patience, I am humbled. I have learned something from everyone.

Most sincere thanks to you for purchasing or just taking the time to read this book. It took a lot of effort to put together these stories and dig up the old pictures after being asked to write about it by this publisher. Many of the photos are over two decades old, and I never imagined they'd end up in a book someday. I would have definitely used a higher-resolution camera or better filming techniques, but that was the furthest thing from my mind back then. In the early '90s, I wrote *Investigating a Haunted Location Handbook* and am currently updating and revising it. Off the top of my head, here are just a few helpful hints and a couple of things you should know before venturing out into the unknown.

If you are delving into the spirit world, it's best to believe in a power greater than yourself. Otherwise, how can any of it make sense? It's like the people who go to church regularly but don't believe in angels, demons, etc. Respect that which you don't know and acknowledge the fact that you don't know what these entities are or what they are capable of. There are good reasons why exorcists have to study their field for years, and will still never know all that there is to know when dealing with the dark side.

The most supernatural book in existence is the Bible. No kidding. It's because of ghost hunting that I was led to read it. All the instructions on dealing with spirits are in there! Beware, though, you may not like what it says. You'll find that if you go back to the Hebrew and Greek denotations of the words by using a Concordance, the words and stories have totally different meanings than what is written. It can guide you through and allow you the Armor of God for spiritual protection. I mean, seriously, if you're going to be seeking out spirits, shouldn't you know how not to lose yourself in the process? Too many people don't take the time to fully prepare for what they will find—or what will find them. And that holds true for any religion.

Now comes the little bit for everyone: if you have a Ouija board, don't break it, attempt to burn it, or toss it in the trash! If it was a gift, don't sell it and don't give it to anyone either. Breaking the board releases whatever you've called up by using it. Also, Parker Brothers made it fire retardant. Discarding it almost guarantees it'll find its way into the wrong hands, and you'll still be connected to it. The easiest way to get rid of a board is to bury it, with a proper ceremony.

Don't go to Dudleytown! It's closed—forever. If you happened to take anything out of there before it was shut down, take that rock, stick, or hunk of moss back to the entrance of Dark Entry or Bald Mountain Roads. Don't worry, it will find its way back up there. Which is true of any haunted place.

Preface

Do not trespass anywhere. I found, in fact, that by asking for permission nicely and professionally, laying out your intentions or what areas you'd like to film, and giving a rough time frame, on paper and in advance, many historic places will welcome you. Always make a donation; every little bit counts in helping places on the historic register to maintain and run these buildings—and get your foot in the door!

If that estate sale you're at is giving you the willies, don't buy anything. If you see things moving out of the corner of your eye that aren't there when you look full on, hands off that vintage Pyrex and leave—now!

Lastly, just a little housekeeping: all photos are collectively copywritten under Cosmic Society/Donna Kent, but individual copyrights are retained by the original photographer. Permission was given at the time of submission to the Cosmic Society website, newsletter, or as part of a formal investigation. I am grateful for your contributions to the field of paranormal investigation.

Photos have not been fabricated or altered in any way except to black out faces for identification purposes. Names and locations have been changed (and confidentiality agreements honored) to protect the privacy and the identities of the people whose homes we were invited to.

If you are interested in purchasing any of my other books, newsletters, or select photographs, you can write to me at donnakent@cosmicsociety.com.

Very Truly,
Donna Kent

And now, this is how it all started.

CONTENTS

Foreword   3

Preface   5

1   Cameras, Cookies, Cosmic Society, and the Not-So-Crossed-Over-Crowd!   13

2   Whoa Nellie!   36

3   Lights! Cameras! Cravings!   52

4   When the Living Haunt the Dead   62

5   In and Out of Owlsbury   70

1

CAMERAS, COOKIES, COSMIC SOCIETY AND THE NOT-SO-CROSSED-OVER CROWD!

1992–2001, STRATFORD, CT

By all appearances, we were a "normal" happy family who had just embarked on building their first home. It was exciting and wonderful watching it all come together into a cute little cape-style house, but something was off from the start. Friends and family members I confided in (some, not all) told me I was overreacting or that the strange little paranormal happenings were just my "morbid imagination," or stress, or dealing with a newborn baby. Anything other than what it really was; what their minds could never accept and much less comprehend. I knew better though, despite their condescension, disbelief, or even well-meaning concern. I knew there was something very unnatural here and began my research into the land we were building on.

We broke ground in 1992 on a vacant lot in a residential area of Stratford, CT. Whatever was unearthed with that first shovel full of dirt, we were unaware of initially, and like any other new homeowners, we photographed all stages of construction and what appeared on film wanted to make itself known.

I was tasked with trying to determine if my interest in the supernatural was causing the other-worldly trouble (as it often does) or if it was this property itself that was plagued with the unrestful dead. Becoming a paranormal investigator has, unsurprisingly, brought me into many haunted dwellings and odd places. I enjoyed investigating and researching these areas, and it has been my choice to do just that. The idea of it takes a different turn when it is *my* home, *my* "safety zone," *my* castle, if you will, that is experiencing the haunting!

I traced the property ownership back only to 1972, which shows the land/lot was named as "Kensington Park," a place for neighborhood children to play ball and congregate. It was sold to a medical practitioner who owned an adjoining lot and building which doubled as a residence and medical business office, where he practiced his trade—and worse. The doctor was arrested twice and finally had his license revoked for molesting his juvenile patients! This was certainly not the news I wanted to hear, but I added it to the file on the property's history as a possible, if not probable cause, accounting for some of the negative energy.

When Secrets Come to Life

A huge yellow orb between the houses. It was most certainly not the moon.

At first it was the exterior of the house that was the hot spot for all kinds of supernatural activity. It was around this time I noticed with regularity that streetlamps would seem to blink off (instead of on) as I drove past them.

The day we excavated the backyard for the swimming pool, Derek found a small antique tonic bottle and silver butter knife in the dirt. I washed them and put them on the windowsill above the sink to dry. Soon after, the knife hurled itself into the stainless-steel basin and continued flying around inside, banging along the edges—around and around it went as if battery-operated! I reached my hand in to stop it but instantly jerked it away as it was burning hot to the touch! Then, as if it never happened, the knife just stopped and dropped to the bottom of the sink. I felt it best to return these items back out into the yard, pronto!

One time while Derek was raking leaves in the same area, he smelled my favorite perfume, yet I hadn't been outside. Later in the day while out tinkering around on the pool mechanicals, the pump stopped working. He got mad and yelled at it and it immediately turned back on and continued pumping (thankfully!).

In the early '90s, the day my son, Justin, was born, the Norwalk Hospital experienced a power outage—during a 110-degree heatwave. To compound matters, the back-up generators failed, and I couldn't wait to leave. From the very first time he was brought inside the house, snapshots of him showed all types of spirit energy. Unfortunately, many of those have been lost to time.

As time went on, so did the entities who kept appearing in the pictures, many times near the children, especially Justin. At this stage, I didn't know anything about spirit photography and discarded many of those early prints and attributed the anomalous images as bad development or that I had absolutely no skill at aiming a camera.

It was dusk on March 19, 1995, when I took the "Mr. Peet" ghost photo. The whole story is chronicled in my first book, *Ghost Stories and Legends of Southwestern Connecticut*, but to summarize, a full-figured man appeared in my film and garnered a lot of media attention, both locally and nationally. Because spirit photography is a form of spirit communication, I had unknowingly allowed permission for this entity to enter my life.

And, of course, like a moth to a flame, having flung that door wide open, it came inside.

Cameras, Cookies, Cosmic Society, and the Not-So-Crossed-Over-Crowd!

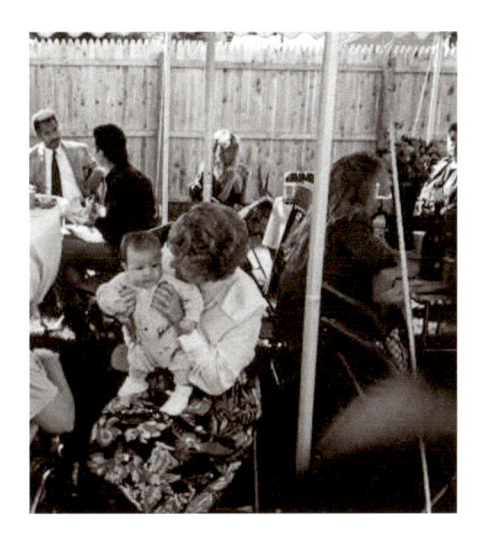

Above left: Chloe and Justin on the living room couch with a strange cloudy white anomaly on the right.

Above right: Friends and family came for Justin's birthday party, where a black blur showed up on film in the lower right. Justin seems to be looking directly at whatever was there.

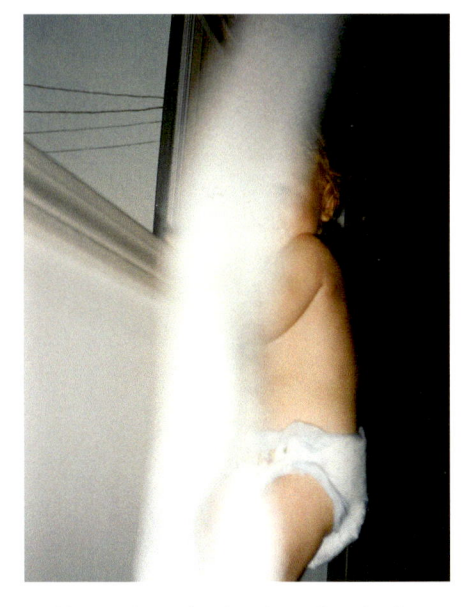

Above left: I thought it was cute how Justin would stand on the baseboard to look out the window, so I snapped two photos. Being 35-mm film and having to wait until after developing, I was surprised to see that the first photo shows black ribbon-like energy. I had no feelings of anything supernatural happening at the time.

Above right: In the second shot, the black energy was replaced by white columns. Could it be that the black is the vortex between the realms that the energy comes through to appear in our world?

When Secrets Come to Life

A zoomed-in view of Mr. Peet from the original shot. He is standing behind the second large tombstone in from the left and has dark hair, a beard and mustache, and is wearing a long black coat.

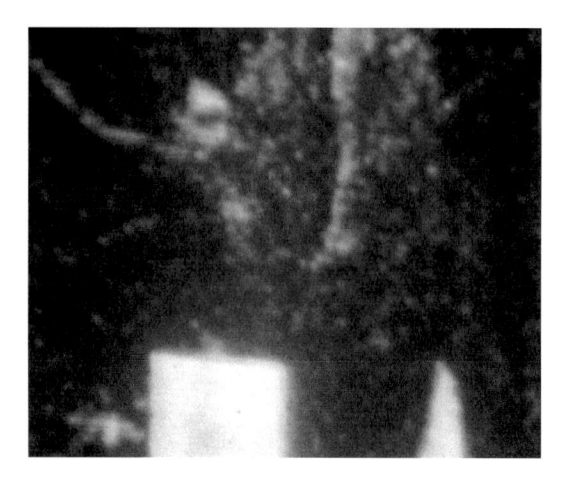

Above left: Here the original is further cropped and zoomed in. This is why it appears less clear, but there is no mistaking that a man's facial image is in the photograph, but his physical body was nowhere to be seen when I took the shot.

Above right: The tombstone of Mr. Peet (also both of his parents) that he was photographed standing behind. Notice the lichen at the base.

Cameras, Cookies, Cosmic Society, and the Not-So-Crossed-Over-Crowd!

Upon further inspection of the gravestone photo, I found that by rotating it 45 degrees to the right, the image of Mr. Peet's face appeared in the lichen, especially when viewed from a distance and in newspaper print.

It was late and the rest of the family was fast asleep. The tea kettle was whistling, and I ran to remove it from the burner before it woke anyone up. Reaching into the fridge for cream, out of the corner of my right eye I saw a "man" standing against the wall where my telephone was, and I could see the phone through his body. He was standing staring straight ahead (not at me), his arms folded and with a very stern expression. His shirt was extremely white and crisp looking. I instantly recognized this man as Mr. Peet from the photo I'd taken at Nichols Farm Burial Ground not more than a month prior. I stood frozen, half in and half out of the refrigerator, as he slowly just faded away and disappeared.

Shaken, I went to sit down in the living room to think through what I had just seen. Just then I heard a clanging noise in the bathroom which was situated in the short hallway between the kitchen and living room. I entered the bathroom to find a small silver cup, which had been placed on the windowsill along with other trinkets, on the floor. Nothing else on the same ledge had been disturbed. Not so for me. I was so rattled that it never even crossed my mind to take any pictures.

Soon after, my then three-year-old son woke up screaming and crying that "The ghost man was in the doorway." On other occasions he would see a young curly haired blonde girl in his room or in the basement. He described her as having "scribbly hair." I saw her once, on the night she followed me home from a graveyard. I had seen a headstone and stood reading the inscription out loud of a four-year-old girl who had passed away in the early 1800s, and in so doing, gave her spirit recognition that probably no one else had in a century or more. Later at home and sitting on the couch, I could see and feel her standing to the left of me. I knew immediately this was the girl from the cemetery, or something impersonating her.

A year or so later, we filmed a national TV show: the ABC special *World's Scariest Ghosts: Caught on Tape*. They brought in a local police sketch artist to draw what Justin described he'd seen. They also enlisted the world-famous psychic James Van Praagh to film and discern with us who or what was haunting our home. The show *Entertainment Tonight* did a segment highlighting the special and compared Justin to

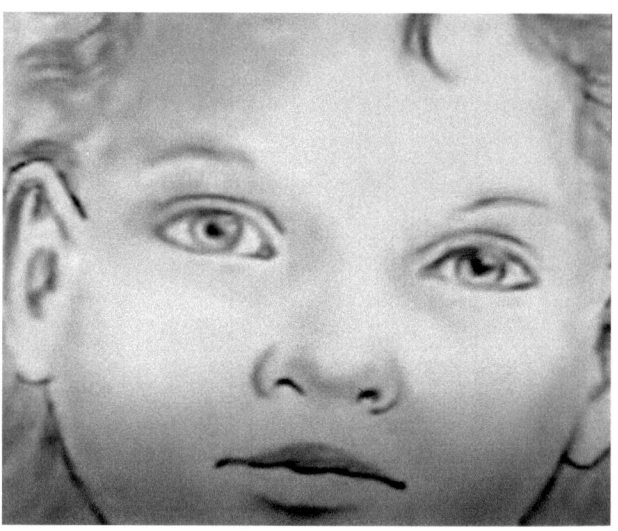

Above left: Police sketch artist's rendition of Mr. Peet as described by Justin and psychic James Van Praagh. The resemblance to the man in the photo from the graveyard is unmistakable. (© *Nash Entertainment*)

Above right: During the filming of *World's Scariest Ghosts*, a Stratford, CT, police sketch artist depicts the "scribbly haired girl" that Justin and I both saw in the home. (© *Nash Entertainment*)

Haley Joel Osment's character in the hit movie *The Sixth Sense* in which his mother finds unexplainable images in photos of her son.

I had, all along, been chronicling the strange events since we moved in. Writing them down each time something happened, even the most mundane things, so I had all those occurrences to share with the TV crew. Some of the incidents were able to be explained away as natural occurrences, or they just plain had an ordinary explanation after everyone in the home was questioned or a logical reason was determined. I crossed those off the list for accuracy. Some of the more memorable and strangely unexplained recollections are recounted here by notes, memory, and photographic evidence.

Spirits, who can easily manipulate energy fields, especially electromagnetic ones, will make physical contact through the five senses, and aside from tasting anything abnormal (exempting my trial-and-error cooking attempts), we experienced them all.

Crazy electronic interferences were just another part of everyday life and left me never knowing whether to laugh or cry when this stuff would happen before my very eyes; VCRs, TVs, computers, and lights all seem to have a life of their own, turning on and off at will, all hours of the day and night. The microwave oven would reset itself and cook nothing. Into the garbage went the toaster oven when it started doing the same. The computer would whir to life as I sat across the room without being manually switched on.

Many times, while watching TV, the kids and I would observe toy ambulances and trucks that would light up and move about the floor at our feet. The batteries had long been removed from most of the toys for this very reason—who needed batteries when they had their own invisible power source? They often came to life while inside the toybox in the basement. Light bulbs would pop or turn on just before I touched the switch.

Speaking of the lights, I spent the day out of town at a friend's house, intending to drive home before the rush-hour traffic, but I was invited to dinner so ended up staying until 8:00 p.m. Derek and the kids had been visiting his family in another state and planned to sleep over. Upon arriving home, I noticed the outside lights, and every single light from the basement to the third floor—inside the closets, little wall socket night lights, and even a pink neon clock that had broken months before—were on inside the house! When I left in the morning, I hadn't turned on any lights, expecting to be home well before nightfall.

Enter the "imps." Dark shadows danced and darted around the corners of the rooms and one time right across the page of a book I was reading. At first, I saw nothing casting these shadows. Same thing with the small, whitish-colored, sparkly ghost lights or a sense of movement out of one's peripheral vision. By the time you turned your head to look, it'd be gone. That was until they started showing themselves. As my perception grew stronger, the ability of these creatures to hide from me weakened. On three such occasions, I'd seen them. The imps differed in height but always had the same sharp and pointy characteristics. They were jet black in color, and they moved lightning fast.

Small items were seen levitating or defying the laws of nature. Chloe and I were making cookies one afternoon, and from the other side of the room we watched a recipe card "lift itself" up and over a slanted dish rack, to float ever so slowly down to the floor.

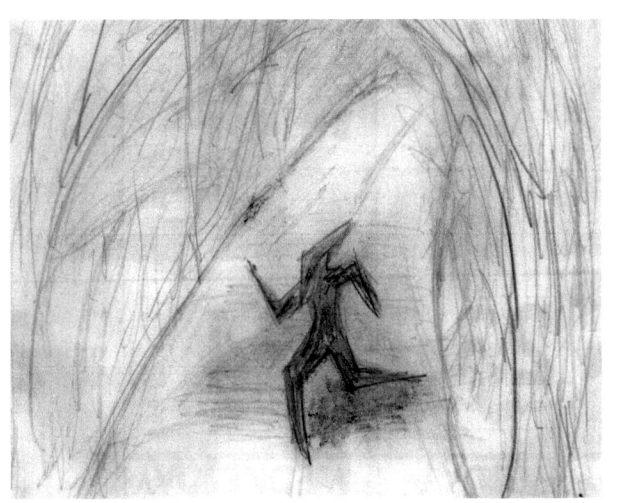

Above left: My attempt to draw one of the imps I saw while driving home one night through a snowstorm. It darted from right to left in front of the car with swift but jerky movements.

Above right: The second sketch of an imp I saw peering out from the dining room doorway. It looked to be about 2 feet high.

Another time Derek was in the kitchen working on a notebook computer. He knocked into a pendant I'd left hanging from a cabinet knob and he watched it "fly down and wrap itself around the phone cord." He called me over, and to both of our disbelief, while trying to untangle this chain, we found it had somehow looped itself so that the phone cord was now inside of the clasped necklace—this could only happen if the phone cord had been unplugged and then inserted inside of the chain. Only a magician with those metal circular rings that they somehow make conjoined would have an explanation for this.

We often heard breathing in our ears or just beside or behind us. We heard laughing or our names being called; either mimicked to match our own voices or ones we couldn't identify. We would hear cries for help coming from a closet in the basement and once from inside my printer but would find nothing. Sometimes we would both hear the same thing, but other times what I heard and someone else did were very different altogether but voiced at the same time. One instance was late at night, everyone was asleep, and Derek and I were awakened to hear a loud noise; I thought it sounded like a large piece of metal being dropped on the kitchen floor, and he thought it sounded like someone yelling through a tube.

Another time, during a blizzard, we heard what sounded like someone breaking into the basement Bilko doors, and upon checking, found no snow disturbed and the doors latched up tight.

We had friends stop over one evening with their toddler and all the kids were dancing in the living room. I snapped a fun photo only to realize after getting the film back that not only was there blue misty energy in it, but when turned upside down, a stark visage of an evil looking old woman can be seen reflected in the mirrored glass of the coffee table. This meant that although unseen to the naked eye, this spiritual mist actually had mass, could be reflected, and cast a shadow. I wondered in astonishment not only what type of intelligence, but its depth and capability to project many images in the millisecond that the camera shutter opens and closes.

The very next day while home alone and talking on the phone, I heard the front door handle turn. I called out, "hold on" and went to check who it was and found the door shut and locked. Upon returning to the call and resuming my conversation, I could clearly hear the same door forcefully swing open and bang against the wall. "What the hell? Hold on a second" I said to my friend and again went to check, only to find the door still closed and locked.

Foul, ungodly smells would permeate a room to quickly be replaced with roses or a floral scent. Doing laundry in the basement once, I got an eerie sensation of being watched. My hair stood on end and goosebumps covered my arms. I felt "something" in the room and smelled an overpowering stench of ozone which was quickly replaced by a strong smell of dill, which I found out was a herb used for protection.

The "events" were becoming somewhat irritating but could still be disregarded to a point; however, we knew this was too much to be considered coincidence and that it was, in fact, paranormal in nature. Standing in the kitchen one night, husking fresh corn for dinner, with our new beagle puppy, Rudy, by my side, something strongly tugged my ponytail, rocking me backwards, and I almost lost my balance. Whipping around thinking my son (who wouldn't have been tall enough to even reach my hair) was playing tricks on me only to find no one there. Rudy growled at the same time, and I quickly found a camera and took his photo.

Cameras, Cookies, Cosmic Society, and the Not-So-Crossed-Over-Crowd!

A friend's baby and my two children were dancing around in the living room. Blue smoky-looking energy can be seen swirling above and around them.

Above left: Examining the photo further, I found that by turning the picture upside down and viewing the mirrored panels in the coffee table, the blue mist is reflected! This means it has mass, it's tangible! Moving so quickly that our eyes don't usually catch it, but the camera does!

Above right: With more scrutiny and enlarging the same area even more, I discovered the disturbing image of a woman's face in the lower right panel. You can see the little boy's head is mirrored in the table where he was standing, but no one was present or standing where this spirit's face appeared. Is it reflected from the mist?

When Secrets Come to Life

A large orb at the front door, just above the chair. Another area of high activity.

Another day, another orb. Here, a small orb is at the edge of the curtain, halfway down the window on the right. The bright light is, of course, just a reflection of the camera flash. "Why small? Why large? Why different colors? Why an orb? Why a mist? Why a full-figured person?" I found myself always wondering and determined to find out.

Cameras, Cookies, Cosmic Society, and the Not-So-Crossed-Over-Crowd!

Rudy had not left his post by the back door. Interestingly, it's as if he has one eye on me and his other eye on the weird grey blur and vortex in the upper right of the photograph.

A disturbing incident happened one afternoon where I almost called the police. The kids and I had been at the town library. Oddly, when we got home, I had trouble getting the front door key to operate and the kids were getting antsy with me to get inside. Finally, it popped open, and the kids ran past me as I now struggled to get the key back out of the lock. They hadn't gotten even halfway across the living room floor when suddenly the sound of a huge crash came from upstairs. They stopped in their tracks, and I assumed it must have been Rudy getting into and knocking over their Easter baskets again. I told them to "Stay right there and don't move" as I started up the stairs to clean up whatever damage had been done. Calling out to Rudy in a stern tone I told him he "was in big trouble." To my shock, Rudy, who had been hiding under an end table in the living room, came crawling out sheepishly. "Uh oh" I thought, "Who the hell is upstairs?" I yelled to the kids to run to our neighbor's house, and they bolted. Rudy crawled back under the table, and I just stood there, halfway up the stairs not knowing what to do.

As if on cue, one of my friends popped her head in through the front door and said "Hey! What's going on? I just saw the kids run next door." I explained what happened and she whipped a buck knife out of her back pocket. "Let's go check," she said without hesitation. I ran back down the stairs and grabbed a carving knife and my camera from the kitchen.

We checked all the rooms on the second floor without finding anything wrong until we reached Chloe's room. I stopped in the doorway to see a large pile of books on the floor in the center of the room, all stacked neatly one atop the other. Another set of books and magazines were found wedged between the side of her bed and the wall. Being a stay-at-home mom, I knew her room wasn't like that when we left.

I've always had a sixth sense, but like any parent of youngsters, it is the sound of silence that can often raise your hackles. One day I stopped vacuuming to answer the

When Secrets Come to Life

Just after the incident in Chloe's room when a loud crash and several books were moved, this (hostile?) red streak was pictured in front of her bookshelf.

tea kettle or something and it hit me; I hadn't heard a sound from Justin. What I did hear was the "GO CHECK NOW" voice in my head. I did, grabbing my camera on the way, only to find him sitting crossed legged on the dining room floor in a meditation position! I snuck up behind him and flashed the camera saying "Hey, whatcha doin' Justin?" He just got up and ran off as if nothing had happened, never answering my question.

One of the worst experiences I've ever had was what's known as the "Old Hag" syndrome. And no, I don't mean just because I've had too many birthdays since these experiences happened! This set of correlated symptoms are explained away by sleep experts as "sleep paralysis," claiming the victim of such is either in a hypnagogic or hypnopompic stage—just on the verge of either falling asleep or waking up. However, they fail to explain the other accompanying phenomena that can happen in accordance with what countless experiencers report. The most common symptoms include total paralysis of the body, hearing noises or sensing a presence in the area, and seeing a demonic-looking figure, usually an old woman, hovering over the face or body.

Early one morning I awoke on the downstairs sofa. My husband and son had also fallen asleep on the other couch. I tried to wake them without success and so I left them there. Alone, I went upstairs and climbed into bed. By now, I felt completely awake and glanced over at the clock which read 4:35 a.m. Just as I was thinking to myself, "I should have just stayed on the damn couch" I heard a noise on the left side of the bed. It sounded like someone rubbing their hands together, but loudly. My hair stood on end as I rolled over to see nothing there. I could hear my heart pounding. Laying on my back now with eyes wide open, I felt "something" press on top of the covers over my chest.

I laid there in shock with my mind racing as I tried to rationalize whatever was happening away and then the pressing happened again. I watched horrified as my puffy goose-down comforter sank towards me from invisible hands! The next thing I knew, I was completely paralyzed; I couldn't speak or move but I could still think and see. I

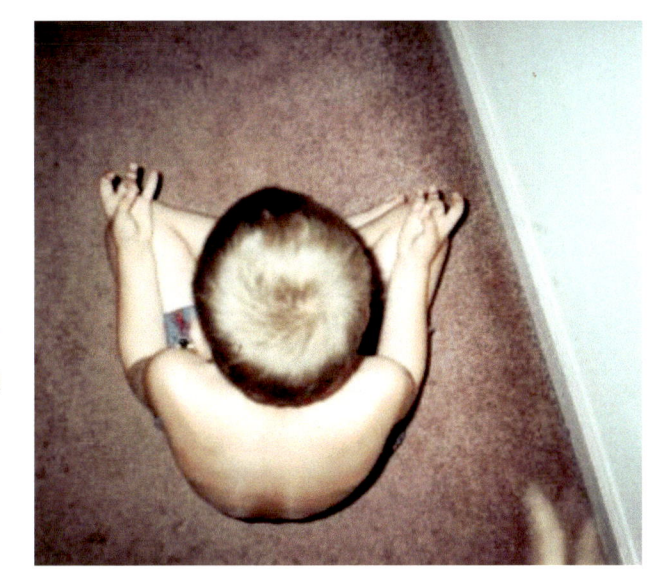

Cameras, Cookies, Cosmic Society, and the Not-So-Crossed-Over-Crowd!

I knew he was up to something, but I never expected to find Justin like this! Legs crossed and fingers posed in a meditative gesture. Did the flash from the camera release him from a trance? I'm unsure of the blur at the lower right. It could have been my own hair, maybe.

knew to try and not show fear and pictured myself laughing at "it." Then, as if watching a movie, I began to see tiny white crosses circling around my body as I lay there and then suddenly the feeling lifted and I was released from being paralyzed (which lasted around twenty seconds but seemed like forever). I immediately fell into a fitful, nightmare rich sleep. The whole thing was downright terrifying, and I never wanted to go through it again. Ever!

This was the straw that broke the camel's back. It was now obvious that a spiritual battle of wills was happening both on the physical realm, as well as the ethereal. I decided I would call in friends and mentors for an official house blessing. While it was quite tense supernaturally, we all felt a noticeable positive shift in the energy of the house once it was over. Things on the home front were quiet, for a little while.

I always knew (not believed) that I was protected, even though I worked my guardian angel's wings to the bone like a tyrant. It was unnerving and always unexpected when the other-worldly things that were witnessed were so unbelievable, and downright impossible to fathom or figure out. They were meant to frighten you, and when you realized that it could stop you in your tracks and often lead to self-evaluation; "Do I really want to be doing this? *Should* I really be doing this?" Ironically or coincidentally, it was always at these junctures that I'd suddenly be requested to document activity on severe cases by clergy of differing sects. Any proof or evidence I might capture on film could possibly be of use to them in determining the validity of the afflicted person's claims and ultimately perhaps, a church sanctioned exorcism. Even though I had come to realize (and experience) the occupational hazards associated with this field, at my own expense, and peace of mind. I was always honored to be asked to help and in return gained invaluable knowledge and trusted mentors.

Speaking of exorcisms (doesn't everyone?), I was invited to be present at one (only as a witness—not photograph) at Our Lady of the Rosary Chapel in Stepney, CT. I sat up in the balcony, having arrived late and midway through the ceremony silently relieved

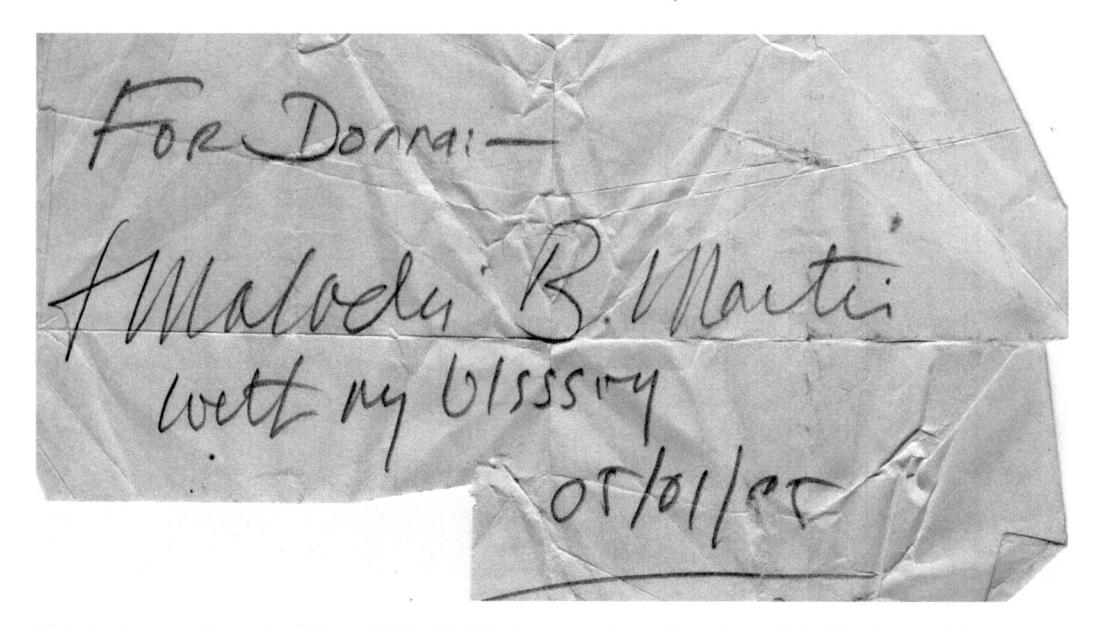

> For Donna:—
>
> †Malachi B. Martin
> with my blessing
> 05/01/9-

This is the note I received from Malachi Martin, exorcist and author of *A Windswept House* and his best-known work *Hostage to the Devil*. One night we had been at a diner discussing an investigation when I wondered out loud about his thoughts on my aptitude for this type of work, but he didn't answer. Later I found this tucked in my pocketbook and I've kept it in my wallet for years. (By the way, the cases with him are those that you'll never hear me speak of or write about.)

and happy to be as far removed as physically possible. What I saw was a person in a white straitjacket (I couldn't tell if a male or female) laying strapped to a gurney in front of the altar. On one side was a team of medical personnel and on the other was a Japanese film crew. At the helm was Bishop McKenna and his aides. To make a long story short, I later learned it was a woman on that gurney—a woman whom I'd met just a few months before at her house during an investigation! She was so ... changed; I didn't even recognize her! As the procedure came to a crescendo with high holy incense filling the air, the lady growled in an unforgettable resonance that had no earthly source. She screamed, spit, growled, snarled, and snapped her head into impossible contortions. It was at this point that the medics called a halt to the ritual claiming that continuing any further would severely affect her health. Believing it had won this battle of wills, the demonic entity then let out an inhuman laugh—one that I can never erase from my mind. It was something I'll never forget. It took several years and exorcisms for her to be delivered.

Not long after, in the early years of Cosmic Society, word of my psychic photography was beginning to be noticed by local media crews, newspapers, and magazines who began to feature my stories and pictures, outside of the scope of fellow researchers and church officials.

It was an overly busy time for the company; an award-winning website was created, and I barely understood how to email. I started publishing a newsletter that went national, while at the same time offering classes and membership programs. I was in the

Cameras, Cookies, Cosmic Society, and the Not-So-Crossed-Over-Crowd!

Grace and Vessels Church service in Danbury, CT. Naiomi Judd was a guest speaker. The first picture is clear.

Seconds later, a huge orb can be seen in front of the cross in the second photo.

An assortment of just a few of the media shows I appeared in or was associated with back in the early days.

A compilation of the initial media articles regarding my work on spirit photography. (© 1990s Stratford Star, New Haven Register, CT Post, Darien Times, etc.)

Cameras, Cookies, Cosmic Society, and the Not-So-Crossed-Over-Crowd!

One of the most popular issues of *Cosmic Connections: The Newsletter of the Cosmic Society of Paranormal Investigation.*

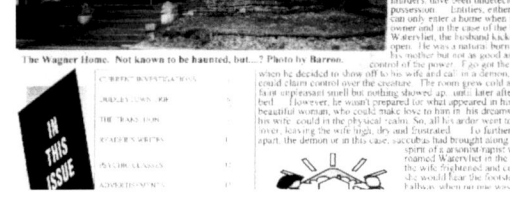

middle of way too many investigations. It was nearly impossible to distinguish which energy or phenomena belonged to which case—or my own house—where much of it would converge. I learned why it's so important not to take on too much at once, but not soon enough.

It was around this time that I was approached by the owner of Haunted CT Tours to become the tour director, and I gladly accepted the offer. Guests would come from all over the nation on pre-packaged tours that could range from a few hours to multiple days. I traveled with groups of all kinds of people to all kinds of spooky locations; we often stayed overnight at historic landmark homes, museums, B&Bs, taverns, and inns. always scouting them out with Cosmic Society first to see if they were indeed complete with ghostly occurrences or spirit activity. I also looked at the structural integrity of the sites for load capacity as some of these very antiquated places just couldn't accommodate the large groups of sixty or more people unless we divided them up into smaller groups and rotated them through attractions or specific areas. I have so many stories and memories of these trips that maybe someday I'll share.

During all this, I was trying to balance family, pets, and home in as normal a way as situationally possible. Luckily, I was gifted with seasoned mentors in the field who taught me the ins and outs of the whos, whats, and whys of each unique situation and how to determine and handle what you're up against.

I experienced, through my own house and those of my clients, nearly every type of "haunted" home. I'd say about half of them are very cut-and-dried; the only thing

When Secrets Come to Life

Just another day at the office.

Above left: There's one in every crowd. Touring skeptics will make sure a "ghost" appears!

Above right: Me on the "Lantern Light Walk" tour that I conducted for over ten years straight in the Old Norwichtown Burial Grounds. Here I'm at the memorial of the DAR (Daughters of the American Revolution) monument. Our first year we expected about fifty people and 300 showed up!

Cameras, Cookies, Cosmic Society, and the Not-So-Crossed-Over-Crowd!

So large were the crowds that the church on the town green opened up for us, and I think they were a bit envious. If only people came on Sunday mornings like this!

lurking is a natural cause, which could happen for any number of reasons—general house noises, bats in the belfry (sometimes literally, other times not, unfortunately), or even mold can cause physical reactions often associated with a spiritual presence: headaches, dizziness, and even hallucinations (which could account for much of what people might think they saw).

The remaining 50 percent had paranormal aspects to them which went from 0–60 in three seconds flat. What the client's energy fed into the situation was critical in determining resolution, and that was as much a wild card as the spirit itself.

I learned a lot about human nature and how people react to the supernatural affecting their lives and the lengths they may or may not be willing to go to deal with it. What was described as an extreme emergency according to the person on the phone was completely de-escalated once we arrived and solutions were introduced which would require work on their part—cleaning up their act in other words—and they weren't always willing to change their lifestyles.

It didn't take long to pick up on the fact that the field of paranormal research and some of the groups were quite competitive rather than wanting to work together to make strides towards understanding and truly helping people. I found that many of the so-called researchers were in it just for thrills, the idea that it was somehow lucrative (it is not) or that they'd become famous overnight. This is not to say I didn't meet and connect with wonderful people and make lifelong friends and associates. No one set of ideals and protocols works for everyone, and it was important to find your "tribe" of like-minded folks. I became quite knowledgeable in choosing the right people for the job at hand. It never failed to amaze me how things worked out; when you needed someone who spoke the native language of the homeowner or who knew the protocols for some esoteric belief system or someone who just happened to have a Bible stashed in their trunk.

We had one case of a lady in Danbury, CT, who mostly experienced things when she laid down in bed at night. She claimed to see creatures emerging from a large mirror

Filming with the cast of *Ghosthunters* at the Carousel Gardens in Seymour, CT.

next to her bed as well as from a closet while she tried to sleep every night. It was only logical after the initial investigation to come back and try to see for ourselves what happened during that time frame. She went to bed as usual, and about five of us sat around her, waiting, watching, and taking photos. We ran video while trying to be as quiet as possible—which is pretty much impossible. It was almost comical how we sat there expecting something akin to skulls flying out of the closet, but the only thing that happened was her turning over in her sleep. Someone's stomach kept growling loudly which couldn't be ignored, nor could we help but chuckle under our breath at how ridiculous we must have looked sitting in a semi-circle around the bed watching her sleep for hours. In the end, though, we did get great photographic evidence and more importantly confirmed to her that she was indeed not crazy and that there was in fact a strong entity at work.

And then came a particularly bizarre investigation (which is entitled "Whoa Nellie!" in this book). The related phenomena started in my own home the night I got the phone call concerning the case specifications. Not to be understated, sometimes they not only follow you home, but before the case is even on your radar, they make themselves known. Such was the investigation of an elderly woman in Shelton, CT.

Cameras, Cookies, Cosmic Society, and the Not-So-Crossed-Over-Crowd!

A large orb on the left in the mirror. Obviously, the flash of the camera is reflected on the right. (© 2001 A. Haley for Cosmic Society)

Above left: The closet door area which caused the homeowner many sleepless nights. (© 2001 D. Burrows for Cosmic Society)

Above right: The second photo in the series is even more distorted and seems to show a black figure on the right—not visible in the first shot. (© 2001 D. Burrows for Cosmic Society)

As it happened, I was in the living room folding laundry when the phone rang. I went to the kitchen to pick it up, and a friend and fellow researcher and I were asked to investigate the demonic activity of a single-family, two-story home. The call lasted about thirty minutes, and I had been given minor details of the distressing situation and odd occurrences that had been plaguing a seventy-one-year-old grieving widow. When the call concluded, I returned to the laundry to find all the previously folded clothes thrown in a jumbled heap in the center of the room. I was so stunned I never thought to snap a picture. Sitting up alone and looking over my preliminary notes on the case, I heard a loud knocking on the wall in the hallway leading from the living room to the kitchen. This would continue throughout the two and a half weeks I was involved, but in different rooms of the house. The knocking became longer, louder, and more persistent. The wall-mounted telephone was constantly manipulated; hangup calls would occur right after the knocking episodes, and the connection between them became too obvious to ignore. A few times I would hear weird growling or snarling sounds coming from different rooms and never a real source. This was sometimes accompanied by foul smells of sweat or old garbage.

On the day of the initial investigation, I was home alone, gathering my notes, checking my equipment and rounding up the supplies I'd need for the overnight visit. Derek called and asked what I was making for dinner, forgetting all about the fact that I had plans that night. "Well," I said as I opened the refrigerator and began looking to see if there was anything easy I could quickly whip up. "For starters we'll use the salad from last night's supper," I said, and placed the container on top of the table. I could only move a few steps in any direction as the phone cord was annoyingly short, so I was limited as to how far I could pace about. Still talking, I turned around and there—without a crash or a sound—was the salad spilled all over the floor with the container balanced perfectly on its side. Where it landed was impossible for it to have just fallen off the table as there was a chair in the way that would have stopped its fall. I quickly took photos and upon development saw two large blurry streaks of energy.

There were numerous other instances of paranormal occurrences that happened at our Connecticut home as the years rolled by and countless other media appearances and interviews. With time and, most importantly, experience, I became knowledgeable on how to deal with unscrupulous journalists and TV producers (a handful—not everybody) whose only goal was to create a segment regardless of the truth (I wrote an article for other researchers as a helpful guideline on this topic). I learned how to manage the supernatural workload by basically leaving the clients' problems outside my own door for the most part, which isn't easy for a natural empath, and certainly takes effort. There are times when, no matter how hard you try, and with the best of protection procedures, some things still try to weasel their way in. There are always variables, being that this is the supernatural, the spiritual, and the unknown. Every case is unique, and there is no one set of rules or magic pill to solve every "haunted" location. Which leads me to the next story.

Cameras, Cookies, Cosmic Society, and the Not-So-Crossed-Over-Crowd!

The salad fiasco happened right around the time I was gearing up for an investigation involving several types of paranormal activity, which included an incubus! You can easily see what appears to be blurry yellowish streaks going up and over the back of the chair—the same trajectory as the container. Then it spilled most of its contents and stayed balanced perfectly while I fetched a camera.

A second angle of the salad container.

2

WHOA NELLIE!

Sunday Driving on the Road to Hell; Fuel No Longer Necessary

FEBRUARY 1996, SHELTON, CT

I didn't like what I'd heard; the details of the case I'd just committed to were at best unsettling and at worst, unsafe. I didn't much like the idea of two women alone in a house with an incubus. Nothing screams sitting ducks louder than that, but there we were, Bonnie and I, and the night had just begun. This was to be my very first "demonically infested" home investigation, and I had no idea how much we weren't told about the situation, which wouldn't be uncovered until around 6 a.m. the next morning.

I was asked to participate in an investigation with a fellow researcher and document anything unusual through audio, video, and still photography in the home of a seventy-one-year-old widow consumed with grief from the loss of her husband. Her name was Nellie, and she tenaciously refused to come to terms with his death; to let go and let him move on to his next existence. And in so doing, she drew him back into her house and her life.

She left his belongings untouched, and his clothes still hung in the closet they shared. The hospital bed, which had been installed for his convenience and comfort, and where he died, had not been removed per Nellie's orders. Not only would she sometimes lie in it to feel closer to him, but she would spend hours sitting alone in the passenger seat of their car, imagining he was still alive and with her. In her mind, he'd drive her to places they'd visited in the past. She would write him heartbreaking letters while sitting there reliving events and locations they'd traveled to.

The haunting wasn't all her fault, however. She was the first guinea pig and a perfect target for the other, more nefarious actors working against the old woman. We're talking about the living, human type of scoundrels. We haven't even begun with the other-worldly scum yet. For one, there was a large piece of land at stake, coveted by her stepson, who, unlisted in his father's will, was conjuring spirits on his own against Nellie in a bid to gain the property by any means possible. This is one of the factors that drew in a demonic presence. It was by no means the only one—but we'll get to that later.

Above left: The doorway to Nellie's bedroom shows a solid black vortex. Just beyond the door is the deceased husband's hospital bed. (He passed two years earlier! But I didn't know that fact, yet!)

Above right: The vortex that "keeps on giving." Here it's moved to the left slightly than the previous shot and so has my camera angle.

Bonnie and I followed the couple in our cars like sheep to the slaughter; unknowing what we were up against as the specifics of the case were purposely withheld. This is understandable to a degree; it is a way to test a person's aptitude towards psychic ability and leave untainted the playing field for preconceived notions. Alas, it is very dangerous in the cases of demonic entities. I have made it a rule within my organization to always inform the team of any type of negative spirits or influences so they have free will to decide if they should in fact join these types of investigations. This was not, however, the practice of these particular researchers. The last thing I was told during the first phone call regarding the case was cryptic and haunting: "Wear a chastity belt!" The elderly man sneered, and with that the phone line went dead.

"What the hell was that he just said? That's not even close to being funny!" I shouted as I slammed the receiver back onto the phone base, only to hear my daughter call out "Mom, you're swearing again!" "Surely, he didn't just hang-up on me," I thought in disbelief, "that'd be so rude!" And then it hit me, no, "It" knew. It knew we were coming and that it would be exposed. It began the campaign against this happening by stirring up all kinds of supernatural happenings in my own home, right after the call ended. I guess this was an attempt to frighten me away. This is a common and predictable *modus operandi*, but not to be downplayed, or in any way underestimated, ever. Demonic forces are insidious and will strike when you are at your most vulnerable and unsuspecting. They don't relinquish their domains without a fight more than most of us are prepared for. But, in hopes of helping Nellie, the battle was on!

It was dusk when we arrived. Once on site, Bonnie and I were led only through the first floor of the house by the elderly "experts" with me, asking as many questions as possible as I hurried along behind them to keep up. They seemed to be in a big hurry to leave. "Where is Nellie, right now?" I asked, as she was obviously not here at her home. "Can you give us any more information regarding this situation? When did you first start working with her?" I persisted. With that last question, I finally got an answer and a strange reaction to it. The senior investigator's wife whipped around like a viper, and although it sounds comical, it was really super weird; at the same time, her body was turning horizontally to face me, I swear it looked like her eyes spun vertically, like a slot machine! My head jerked back in an automatic reaction—what the heck was I looking at? I caught something I still can't explain. She realized it too and quickly recovered herself and replied "Oh, we've only known her for about two weeks, right dear?" She nudged her husband with her elbow, who stepped in and concurred they'd gotten a phone call from Nellie less than a month ago.

We were specifically warned not to enter the basement without any explanation. I had no reason to doubt them at that time, but I found it a bit shady how our questions were basically ignored, and hardly any, even general, info on the paranormal activity had been shared with us. As if reading my mind, it was then that they suddenly had to go. Both made a quick turnabout and headed back to the front door. We'd been there less than two minutes, and the demonologists were bolting. Strangely enough, as we all walked back through the hallway from the kitchen to the main living area and front entryway they were rushing to, Bonnie noticed something on the floor and stopped to pick it up—rosary beads. We looked at each and both said in unison, "That wasn't there a second ago." As we stopped and glanced around for a probable cause, it dawned on each of us: it was impossible not to see that within an arm's reach of nearly every angle of the home (except the hallway) was some type of religious icon, statues of the Virgin Mary, palms, or other representations of her faith. It was a Roman Catholic overload. All that was missing was the confessional, the organ, and the stained-glass windows. I was half-expecting a nun with bleeding eye sockets to pop out from behind a doorway at any moment. I think I muttered, "Oh dear God!" under my breath in my shock of not noticing this before, and without stopping, the craziness progressed.

Left to our own defenses (literally), we did what we always do on an investigation (minus the occupants-on-camera interview since we were not told where she was, or if she'd return). We unpacked all our equipment on a completely cleared-off dining room table. This helps a person like me have a home base for all our stuff and stay organized so the equipment could be accounted for. The dining room felt "okay" but not great; it was dimly lit solely from the windows, which showed only the last glimpses of twilight from outside. I could feel something was really "off" with this place but tried to remain neutral about it and experience what was there. Whatever that might be. We'd been there less than a half-hour.

Above left: Black vortex on left at Nellie's clothes closet.

Above right: In the second frame, the black portal has expanded and covers any sign of the wardrobe interior. Little did I know at the time just what had transpired in this closet.

"Onward and upward Bon," I said, trying to sound upbeat as I headed towards the staircase to the second story, cassette recorder in hand. We proceeded to place these and other devices upstairs and went back down to the first floor. We checked our watches and noted that the tapes would have to be flipped over in about an hour and then repeatedly with fresh tapes. I decided it was long past time for a cigarette break, so we headed outside to let our equipment run without any noise from either of us.

Outside was wonderful compared to how it felt inside, and the difference was immediately noticed by both of us. The outside felt safe, or safer, at least, than the vibe within. On the physical level, the interior had that "old lady," old clothes, geriatric, and medicinal sort of sickening smell mixed with undertones of some God-awful perfume well past its expiration date. We could tolerate that for one night.

We took exterior photos of the home, the little garage, and the shed and headed around to the backyard. That's when we saw it. Several yards back there was a small light coming from a house trailer. Next, we heard it; faint rhythmic music or some sort of cadence of sounds that we couldn't understand or make out. No one told us anyone else was on the property, inferring we were alone, never pointing out that a trailer with an unknown occupant was present. "Hmm," Bonnie said, "we'll have to go check that out at some point tonight," making it clear she was certainly the braver of the two of us.

Back inside, I started noticing how only the living room felt "safe." Not that it felt good by any means, but much better than any of the other rooms. It was closest to the front door and, if necessary, escape! The heaviness in the house was stronger than it was just an hour earlier. The atmospheric tension was becoming increasingly noticeable and uncomfortable. The darkness outside was now being mirrored within. It was time to flip the tapes, and we did so, snapping photos along the way. Little did we know what we had captured on film and that it was following our every move throughout its domain.

Like any investigation, we sat, we waited, and we watched, talking in whispered tones about what we knew about Nellie and her experiences, which wasn't much. However, Bonnie was a life-long Shelton resident, and she knew a lot of people. She'd heard some stories about this area.

The house bordered a working farm and high-tension transmission towers were pretty much on the plumb line of the two lots. As the story goes, one day, the fourteen-year-old neighbor was playing around with a small group of friends of roughly the same age. Perhaps he was showing off or just being silly, but he climbed up on the rungs of the tower; nearing the top, his wristwatch connected with and sparked a power line. His hand was blown off, he fell to the ground, and he died. "Wow, what a way to go! And so young!" I said with a knot in my throat. We discussed what kind of energy that untimely death in addition to the towers themselves could be bringing into Nellie's place.

We sat in the bedroom shared by Nellie and her dead husband's now empty hospital bed to see what impressions we'd pick up, if any. It was suddenly very hot in the room and was becoming stuffy, making it hard to breathe. We noted this and wondered if maybe these were some of the conditions the husband had suffered from. I felt a strange electric sort of tingling on my head, and Bonnie snapped a picture which showed three white dots above my head. Unfortunately, this picture has been lost. Bonnie mentioned suddenly that she was not feeling good. "Gonna be alright, Bon?" I asked, and she just shrugged and said, "Not really."

We continued sitting quietly for a bit longer, just taking in the energy of the room and our impressions of it. Akin to a thunderclap, the gong of the grandfather clock in the living room struck midnight and nearly gave both of us a heart attack. After shaking our heads and getting over the shock, we laughed it off in recognition of our anxiety and nerves and relaxed a minute, thankful for the much-needed comic relief. It was a short-lived reprieve.

The next thing we heard was the sound of heavy footsteps on the floor above us. "Uh oh, here we go," I whispered and wished I was anywhere else in the world but here. Outside smoking a cigarette would be like a dream vacation right now.

I didn't want to go up there. I had to, though, because it was my turn to flip the tapes. I bit my lip, rolled my eyes, shook my head, and took a deep breath. Whatever was up there, I could already feel it from down on the first floor. My feet felt like lead weights as I made my way up each step, snapping off pictures, using the flash to light my way as the hallway light was (incredibly) not working anymore. Claustrophobia hit me hard as I climbed the stairs and felt squeezed into a small space, although it was just an average-sized staircase. I learned later when viewing the photos why this happened.

Whoa Nellie!

Right: White, blue, black, and gray mist in the hall where the doorways to the workroom and bathroom are located.

Below: High-tension wire towers.

Above left: White/gray mist at the doorway to Nellie's bedroom. Notice the black at top again.

Above right: Slightly different view of the doorway to the couple's bedroom with a similar white/black pattern of energy.

I was surrounded on each side by spirit energy! The white being the earthbound spirit, perhaps Nellie's husband trying to protect me from the dark energy opposite. No wonder I felt crowded! This was nothing compared to what would happen next.

Steeling myself, I went into the first room on the right at the top of the stairs. The sensation of being in the presence of pure evil was unlike anything I'd ever experienced before. If you've ever been in that type of situation, you know exactly what I mean. If not, count your blessings. There are no words to describe it, especially when it's your first time. It permeates your entire body, mind, and soul, and that's a pale cliche. With time and experience, it doesn't get any better, but with faith and belief in a higher power, you become stronger and realize the protection against such entities. It doesn't happen overnight, and for some, it doesn't happen at all. Some never recover.

I dreaded walking in any further than the doorway, but the recorder was on a table across the room, which wasn't even large, but to me, in that situation, it might as well have been miles away. I hit the camera for the flash to find it and luckily all I had to do was turn the tape over and pop it back in. Working in pitch darkness and as fast as

Whoa Nellie!

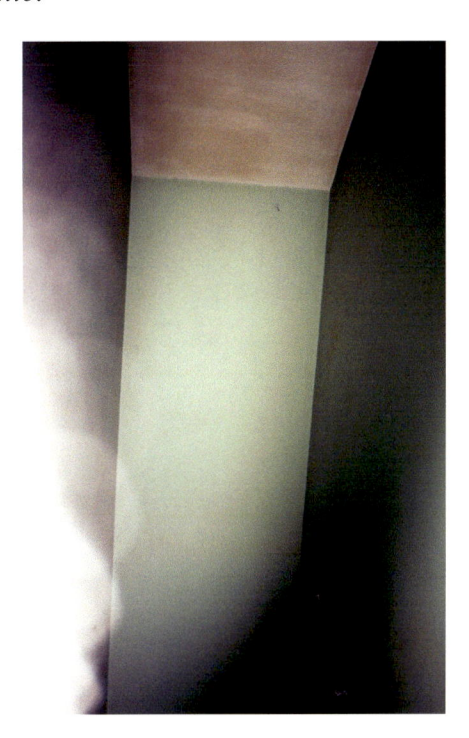

A weird angle of the staircase that I always dreaded climbing to the second floor, showing what look to be "opposing" forces; white on left and black on right.

possible with every instinct inside me yelling "RUN, GET OUT OF HERE!" Seconds seemed like a lifetime with whatever else was there, and I realized how badly my hands were shaking! Finally, I finished fumbling around with what should have been the simplest of tasks.

I took one step towards the door and suddenly, like a bat out of hell, something small, black, and screeching flew out from under the bed and hurled itself down the entire set of stairs, smashing full on into the wall below. It leapt up and off the smaller landing at the bottom and flew off to the right, exactly where Bonnie was standing. I don't even remember getting down the steps, but I do remember screaming "What the flying #! @% was that?" From Bonnie's perspective, it must have been crazy, seeing, at eye level, "an airborne cat that was in wild animal mode, like the hounds of hell were after it, terrified out of its mind." We never saw it again. Just another thing no one ever mentioned to us, about pets being in the house. I still haven't decided who was more shocked, us or the cat!

It was at this point we needed to get outside to clear our heads. I needed a cigarette. Make that three. All at once. I offered one to Bonnie, knowing full well she didn't smoke. Bonnie said she was going to be sick and turned towards the front door. I grabbed my lighter and the car keys and followed her. We decided to put a little bit of distance between us and the house, and coffee would provide us with some relief!

Bonnie puked over by the shed. She quickly gathered herself up and we left for Dunkin' Donuts. As we drove, Bonnie asked, "Are you smelling that?" I looked over at her and answered, shaking my head, "No, nothing weird." She was literally gagging and fully opened the window, saying, "I can't believe you can't smell it! Oh my God! Open

This black vortex is what was captured on film as I entered the upstairs bedroom, using only my camera's flash for light.

all the windows! It's like rubbing alcohol! It's SO strong!" She struggled to breathe, and I didn't smell a thing except a little car exhaust as we had by now reached the drive-thru at the coffee shop.

The smell left as quickly as it had come, and Bonnie was feeling a little better. By the time we got our coffees, she was fine, and we headed right back. We were gone fifteen minutes tops and had our "second winds" for the hours that lay ahead. All light-heartedness disappeared as my car crept into the pitch-black driveway and the house's familiar feeling of dread formed a knot in my stomach.

The safe cozy feeling of being in the car and in the normalcy of the "real" world was too short-lived. I stalled a bit, putting up the windows one at a time and gathering up the pocketbooks, donuts, etc. Leaving me in the dust, Bonnie was out of the car and making her way to the backyard, and there was no way I was going to let her go alone. I piled everything I just collected and placed it on the hood of the car. Catching up to her, we tiptoed across the field to the edge of the trailer and she whispered, "Might as well get this over with while we're out here." "Yeah, thanks for the warning, pal," I said sarcastically, and we both snickered. As we approached, the sounds we'd heard earlier were now much higher pitched and frenzied. Someone was chanting! The voice was deep and guttural, it was male and sounded like an incantation. Here or there I'd make out the name of some underworld deity, but barely more than that. This was a summoning.

The information provided later stated that this was where Nellie's outcast stepson lived. Allegedly, he felt betrayed and openly coveted the house and the ever increasing in value, nice-sized acreage. He felt it was his inheritance and should have been left to him, not her! His "workings" against her and towards his own benefit would explain part of the puzzle of why we were dealing with more than just the spirit of his father, Nellie's husband. We didn't stick around that trailer for long, thank God, but gleaned valuable information just by what we'd heard. Tragically, he and his witchcraft were by far not the worst wickedness that would befall poor Nellie.

We went back inside to recorder duty and spent some time in the other rooms. I was drawn to the closet that still held all the husband's clothes. Nellie couldn't bear to part with them or any of his possessions; oh no, that would make her feel as if he was really gone, really dead. At this point, I had no idea how long it'd been since he died. This would be another bit of surprise data that we'd learn more on in the morning, as well as how a closet in the house would come to figure prominently, towards Nellie's further mental and spiritual descent.

We could both feel the husband's energy very strongly in his work studio. He was a ham radio enthusiast, and this was his domain. He was proud of it, and he had many good times in this room. There was a quality to his spirit that was kind and protective. I think he worked overtime on our behalf that night. He presented himself on film as a white, almost cloudlike form, but with a distinct pattern (I coined it the "thermal underwear design" for lack of anything better and because that's what it looked like); the pattern showed movement, an oscillation.

Thinking about that, I tried to calculate the speed of that movement; how far did it travel or what space did it cover in the fractional time of the camera shutter? So, the area with energy would have to be measured, let's say 5 feet, like from "this wall to that

The husband's closet was not exempt from the black portal/vortex.

When Secrets Come to Life

A ghostly mist appears on the left in the workroom of Nellie's husband where he would communicate with the outside world.

chair" for example. Using the shutter speed info and doing the calculations, it appeared these entities were moving at around 600 mph! That's why we don't normally see them with our physical eyes, but the camera does!

Bonnie and I (and that poor cat!) were the only witnesses to what happened in the harrowing ten hours we spent there, but we did have the hard copy proof through our photographs and later having both the pictures and negatives analyzed. We never found any evidence on our cassette tapes of EVP (electronic voice phenomena) that I can recall.

It just so happened (by no coincidence) that Bonnie worked at a camera store, and I wondered if I could pick her boss's brain on a few related things since much of what we did relied on our photography. I had heard somewhere that there was a way to convert a normal camera into infrared mode, a spectrum of light the normal human eye can't perceive. "There is a way," he said, "but instead, why don't you just try putting a piece of red film, like plastic wrap or the kind used for Easter baskets, over the flash? Let me know what happens." I agreed but almost forgot all about it until about 3:30 a.m. when I applied a small piece of red plastic taken from a pair of 3-D glasses you'd get at a movie theater. I was stunned a few weeks later when I got the photos developed and made it a point to return to the camera shop for the owner's assessment. I'll never forget his reaction.

For some reason I had the film developed somewhere else as it was a less expensive option. Anyway, first he asked to see the negatives as well as the prints. I had taken seven rolls of film, and I believe I got about fourteen pictures depicting anomalous images; white mists, black "funnels" or vortexes, and other types of spirit energy. Interestingly, to us both, one roll was completely black—this usually indicates over-exposure or too much light. It can even happen if exposed to radiation (are spirits a form of radiation? I think so. Why else would we use a Tri-Field Meter to detect them?). But wait, there in the middle of the roll of all the pitch-black shots was one single image which showed Nellie's kitchen (throwing the over-exposure explanation out the window).

The clock on the wall displayed the time of morning to be 3:35 a.m. The entire shot is red except for outlines of appliances and details such as the clock and the cabinet handles. But on the right side of the frame is a white and gray mass, a cloudy looking mist that seems to have that familiar pattern to it, as has been seen in other photos taken that night. Yet in this one, a hooded figure appears just behind the mist! The store owner, after comparing the negatives to the photos, gave me a side glance as he held the photo at arm's length (as if distancing himself from it) and said "Donna, this is an impossibility! EVERYTHING in this picture (except for the black outlines) should be RED! There is no natural cause for the white area in this picture!"

This was the fourth time my pics and negatives had been expertly analyzed and found to have no outside manipulation, no trickery, no shenanigans, no reflections, refractions, or light leaks. They had no normal cause or explanation. They could not be debunked. Which meant, proof-wise, this shit was real.

Back to that night at the house, it was about 4:30 a.m. when she said it. I knew Bonnie and I knew this would happen. She jumped up and proclaimed, "Let's go down to the basement!" "No way!" I yelled. Every bone in my body screamed, "Oh hell no!" I was not going down there. "Well, I am!" she continued, and down she went. I couldn't watch, and suddenly all the coffee kicked in and I had to pee, bad.

Going in that bathroom alone while she was in the forbidden basement was beyond unnerving! It was like the walls had eyes. Not good anywhere but especially the

Above left: The kitchen shot where I had tried using red film over the flash. There was no one else in the room when I took this. There's something about red lenses that allows one a peek into the spirit world. Maybe that's why the military only uses green night vision now? There've been multiple reports.

Above right: The grayish black vortex appeared in front of the archway to the bathroom door.

bathroom! Nothing happened outwardly, but the room seemed to mess with your mind. It was a long corridor past the tub and opposite the vanity. I avoided looking at the mirror as best I could. The toilet was way at the end and around a privacy corner. I could feel something right behind me and I held my breath waiting for the shower curtain to jiggle or rip open at any second. "Next time, I'll go outside" I thought and got out of there as fast as possible.

Bonnie was now coming up from the cellar, and I was relieved to see her, still all in one piece. "No coffins or mangled hands reaching for you down there?" I joked, raising one eyebrow, and she reported that nothing unusual happened or that she perceived otherwise.

We pretty much stayed in the living room for the rest of the duration until the first peek of light. It was time. We thought about packing up our gear as we finished the last drops of coffee. We thought it was over. We were so wrong!

It was after 5 a.m., and we headed to collect the equipment strewn about the dining room table. We wound cord, labeled tapes, etc., and packed it all up. I swear the table was cleared of everything. I felt the top of my head—yup, my glasses were there. We were good to go. I turned around to do the once-over glance of the room before heading out and finding, out of thin air and sitting smack-dab dead center of the table, a large Ziplock bag. My mouth hung open and I turned back to Bonnie who was already at the front door and said, "Is this your bag?" She had no idea what I was talking about and, seeing my expression, came to look. "It's not mine," she said, shaking her head. My heart was pounding, and it wasn't from the coffee. I was stunned and remember asking Bonnie, "Should I open it?" I'm not in the habit of going through other people's things, and it felt awkward. And then she said "Yeah, what are you waiting for?"

Well, well, well. Now it was my turn to shake my head. The first thing I pulled out was Raymond Moody's book *Reunions: Visionary Encounters with Departed Loved Ones* (New York, NY: Villard Books, 1993). I recognized it immediately; I had just read it a month before after spotting it in the library. "Why in the world ... would she have this? Be reading ... this?" I questioned, and Bonnie looked up and said "They gave it to her! They set her up!"

To briefly summarize, Moody was a researcher into NDEs—near-death experiences and the afterlife. The book detailed his work on spirit communication, specifically a "Psychomanteum." Ancient Greek beliefs held that if you gazed into a shiny, reflective surface, you could contact the dead. Scrying or mirror gazing, same idea.

Next out of the bag was a small journal, and out of it tumbled a stack of papers, bound with an overstretched rubber band. We turned to the journal first; this was the collection of love letters. Handwritten messages of despair and nostalgic longings, obsessively one-sided conversations that Nellie had penned, alone, out in the car. She could not and would not fathom that he was really gone. And she wrote all about it. She thought she caught a glimpse of him or heard his voice call out a couple of times. These were moments of bliss for Nellie, and she wanted more. More time with him. She searched high and low to find the source of what she thought were his attempts to reconnect and yet she always ended up alone. Utterly alone. She started to become obsessed with contacting him directly. She was blinded to any danger or repercussions that could occur. Nellie now had a reason to have hope.

Except, there was one big problem. Something other than her deceased spouse was crawling into bed with her at night! I'll spare everyone the mental graphics and say that this went on sporadically and became violent. Nellie had noted in the journal that she was flung across the room, crashing into a chair, breaking her arm and banging her head, and it was at that point that she finally reached out for help. Or so she thought.

Bonnie unwound the packet of papers, and I turned away from the journal to look. We saw invoices and receipts of every shape, size, and denomination from the "experts" to Nellie for her payments to them. They included (but were certainly not limited to) hundreds of dollars spent for them to buy and place a statue of a saint upside down at the gravesite, the materials/labor and "expertise" to construct a psychomanteum in one of Nellie's closets (this included stapling black garbage bags to line and darken the walls), and other similar "metaphysical service" type charges. Now it was my turn to feel like I might puke. They had led her to use the spirit communication device, and knowing her willingness to try anything, she was fair game. Not to mention she was a desperate, vulnerable, and wealthy widow to boot.

Even if one was to follow the explicit instructions in Moody's book regarding the safest methods for use, such as fasting while praying and ruminating for days on the person you want to connect from the other side, every situation is different, there are so many life factors to consider before ever even thinking about doing this. You must consider every possible scenario and be prepared for the consequences. Heck! I was learning that just being there as a researcher! Nellie jumped at the opportunity to try it, but she never recorded in the journal whether she had ever actually saw or had been reacquainted with her husband's spirit by using the device, as she sat in a closet, in a big comfy chair, slightly reclined, and with her feet up. Positioned about 3 feet off the floor was a large mirror and behind it a very dim nightlight.

What was penciled into the journal was more incidents happening than just the incubus now and she was terrified to be in her own home (obviously her cat was too!). But what bothered me at that moment was reading the dates on the receipts—June 1994 and upwards. So apparently these people had lied right to my face and had not been "working with Nellie for less than a month" prior. No, they'd been bilking her for two years continuously and now the situation with whatever was literally beckoned and allowed to enter the house through a spiritual gateway was well beyond control.

It was the same year, 1996, that the movie *The Frighteners* (a Universal Pictures supernatural comedy horror film directed by Peter Jackson and co-written with Fran Walsh) was released starring Michael J. Fox wherein the "exorcist" works in cahoots with the ghosts to extract a fee from the "haunted." I couldn't help but make general comparisons to this case. The playbook sure had its similarities. Gee, thanks "experts" for all the "help."

Within days, I confronted them about it in front of the entire group. I wanted to know why they lied to me. What was with the obsession of what I'd called their "traveling psychomanteums" all over the place? (They had done this in several locations, I'd discovered, to the unsuspecting, some as young as teenagers.) "Why all the deception?" I pushed for answers. "Why this, why that and how could you?" I was mostly polite, and I didn't swear, but everyone could tell I was serious, nor was I going to let the matter slide. My question was met with a twenty-minute totally unrelated story about bike riding in California and once the old guy finally stopped to take a breath, I raised my hand again and said, "That's all well and good but you still didn't answer any of my questions about Nellie, and what went on there…"

There was a huddle and suddenly the meeting was pronounced adjourned. The geriatric duo was quickly surrounded by their damage control groupies and shuffled off the premises. A couple of days later I received, by registered mail, basically a cease-and-desist order. I was labeled "disruptive" and ordered not to return. As if I would! I had made up my mind the morning of the investigation at 6 a.m. at Nellie's that I wouldn't be a part of their scam, so it didn't take a psychic or a form letter to keep me away or to know I was done with them.

Bonnie and I hadn't been the first set of investigators in that wretched place. No, that trio (who never got a shred of evidence on film) told us they'd all brought their pajamas and went to bed! (WHAT? In a house with a known incubus!) And that they'd all (so conveniently) had psychic dreams that connected to Nellie and her house. None of what I'd heard them proclaim ever came to pass, or it was a blatant rehash of information already released to those of us who were involved in the case, which was nil. "Dreams," that proved absolutely nothing, but duly noted, nonetheless.

Whoa Nellie!

One of the many "traveling psychomanteums" set up at a restaurant with crowds of overzealous researchers, teenagers, and the general public, clamoring for a turn in the little cubicle. You can see the shiny black garbage bags that had been stapled to the walls and the white energy on the left side of the photo.

Nor were we the last. I remained friends with many of the members of the group and they relayed what had transpired after I was no longer affiliated; the threesome that followed us were independently "overtaken" to differing degrees. One said she had become transfixed by patterns of morphing, wicked-looking faces on the ceiling in Nellie's bedroom. She could feel herself losing the power to turn away. Another had lapsed into a trance state and was non-communicative. The final and probably the stupidest move by the third member included doing religious provocation (only to have it backfire) which would compel a reaction from the spirits. He wore around his neck and hoisted into the air an enormous wooden cross (think rapper Flavor-Flav's clock necklace) while shouting profanities and defamations at the top of his lungs (think Flav's lyrics!). As if that wasn't enough, he further snapped by guzzling entire bottles of holy water, frantically raiding his glove box for more after devouring what he could find in Nellie's stash. From what I've heard, the poor guy's never been the same since. I know it sounds comical visualizing it, but in reality, it wasn't funny. It was a very educational example of what can, would, and does happen to people who attempt to take on the spirit world with the wrong intentions or capacity to deal with it. I thank God for the bullets I dodged by removing myself from that crowd. And from that house.

I saw Bonnie recently to pick her brain on any points I might not have remembered and to make sure I'd gotten all my facts straight—after all, it's been more than twenty-five years since this all transpired. The last she knew, and this was a few years back, Nellie was still in the house and refused an offer from Bonnie's husband who wanted to buy the land. When he mentioned that his wife had been part of the "situation" she had at the house, she flatly denied any knowledge of what he was talking about and abruptly ended any further conversation by pretty much slamming the door in his face.

In the end, I'd like to say I was thankful for the experience, but I'm not sure that'd be true.

3
LIGHTS! CAMERAS! CRAVINGS!

Cats in the Sky and Monkeys on Your Back!

December 1996–1998, Bridgeport, CT

I was starving and debating whether it was worth ordering take-out, but with Christmas around the corner, the budget forced me instead to heat up mystery leftovers. Sitting down to eat, the phone rang. "It figures!" I thought, fighting down the urge to answer the phone with an off-the-cuff remark. "Mm hmm, hello?" I said, with exaggerated politeness. The voice replied, "Hello, this is Tammy from the Sci-Fi [now branded Sy-Fy] Network's *Sightings*, is Donna Kent available?" Simultaneously, I changed my tone and lost my appetite!

My mind raced back to the previous week when I had sent the show a copy of my 1997 Ghost Calendar which had just been pre-released in time for next year's sales. "Donna, I love your calendar" she said, and before I knew it, we'd been on the phone for an hour! Reciprocal calls and conversations ensued, while Tammy compiled a proposal for the producer's approval. The wait was tough, although not lengthy. They soon approved a seven-minute segment concerning my calendar, photographs, and line of work.

Filming would begin the following week, December 16, 1996, as the *Sightings* production season was about to end in two weeks, so it was now or never! The producer inquired about my family, work, equipment, and any current investigations I was involved with. Due to the holiday season approaching, my team and I were on a kind of hiatus, sticking to local historic sites, foregoing travel to stay close to home. There was one ongoing case we had been pursuing on an on-again/off-again basis. Intrigued, *Sightings* wanted details.

A woman, Hazel, her boyfriend, Ike, their new baby, and a myriad of pets were renting the first floor of a two-family dwelling in Bridgeport, CT. The neighborhood mainly consisted of run-down two- and three-family rental apartment houses wedged between public-assisted housing projects, infamously labeled "Father Panik Village," and one of the city's highest priced real estate markets, the ultra-wealthy waterfront

Lights! Cameras! Cravings!

Right: HOUSE FRONT ORBS, 2ND VISIT, COSMIC SOCIETY INVESTIGATION TEAM: During the formal investigation, a team member photographed several orbs at the left front of the residence. (© 1998 R. Dowding for Cosmic Society)

Below: HOUSE FRONT SMOKY, 2ND VISIT, COSMIC SOCIETY INVESTIGATION TEAM: Different camera, different investigator, same night. Now the energy has progressed from orbs to what looks like a white mist near the front of the house. Had that cluster of orbs now gathered enough energy to project itself like a mist? (© 1998 C. Milano for Cosmic Society)

mansions in a section of town named "Saint Mary's by the Sea." A mere few blocks in distance were all that separated these three distinctly different areas. If ever there was a "twilight zone" of personalities, societal class structures, and privileges (or lack thereof), this was it!

I informed the producers of the paranormal occurrences Hazel relayed to me; most notable were the reactions and behavior changes of the pets who appeared at times to be deeply disturbed by invisible forces. Candles would "jump out of their holders" landing several feet away, hearing a loud crash of dishes falling in the kitchen and upon inspection finding nothing amiss, also hearing her jewelry box open and close without cause. There were constant phone problems that repairmen could never explain. Tammy got a taste of this phenomenon when trying to call me from California and hearing my phone say it was disconnected. Then dialing Hazel's number only to hear the exact same message over and over. Finally, she resorted to having the operator assist who got through without incident. (This was an old trick from back when the world actually had a live person answer when you dialed "O" for an operator! None of us had cell phones!)

Minor things became bigger annoyances as happens during the "Infestation Stage" of a haunting, and as could almost be predicted, things soon progressed to the "Oppression Stage" where the outside force can no longer be ignored or written off to any natural occurrences. The actualization and realization of the phenomena now becomes scary and then problematic—which is, of course, the preferred response in terms of the entities who are manipulating and helping to control the energies generated by the occupants, now called the "Obsession Stage."

Progressing beyond the pets, Ike began exhibiting personality and behavioral changes, and his drinking became an issue of contention between the couple. Due to his drunk evenings and morning hangovers, Ike was late to work or not going in at all. People can be insidious in their own right, even without the influence of the supernatural. All of their bad habits, addictions, and dirty little secrets will sneak out to see the light of day every once in a while. With the persuasion of an ill-intentioned spirit, these issues will become amplified, intensified, and finally a dominant force in the person's life. Negative spirits have a cruel knack of exacerbating and expounding on troubles that can seem insurmountable, and they thrive on literally sucking whatever joy once existed into thin air. Strings of bad luck or just everything seeming to go wrong kept happening with no end in sight. Bickering, nagging, arguments, and shouting tirades became the norm. He was fired from his construction job, causing further stressful financial problems for a struggling couple with a newborn baby.

I relayed to the producers how after one particularly trying night for Hazel, I offered to take her out to dinner—it would be the first time in three months she had left the apartment and the baby in Ike's care, and she was more than hesitant about the idea. I told her it would do her good to get out, if only for a short while. She relented, but on the condition that we go to a restaurant just around the corner from her house. She was worried and uncomfortable for the entire twenty or so minutes we were out, and it was obvious she'd rather be home. I drove us back, and it was then that I personally witnessed something strange happen and began right there and then to document the incident.

I informed the production team that I and a few different Cosmic Society crews had surveyed and probed the site on three or more occasions, and that most times I had

HOUSE SIDE CLEAR, 1ST NIGHT: Hazel and I stood outside facing the right side of the house and talking when suddenly we both saw something different happen in the lower window area. This prompted me to start photographing the area. Nothing abnormal had shown up in the film at this point.

HOUSE SIDE SMOKY, 1ST NIGHT: Seconds later, the next photo in the series shows white smoky-looking spirit energy just above the window area that had captured our attention. For the record, no one was smoking, and the temperature wasn't low enough for "hot breath on a cold night" to be photographed.

When Secrets Come to Life

HOUSE SIDE SMOKY, 1ST NIGHT: Here, I've again experimented with the red film over the camera flash. A smoky mist was captured as in other photos in the same area and taken minutes, if not seconds, apart.

CAT FACE, 1ST NIGHT: A blue diaphanous mist configured itself into a clear image of a cat's face in the air above the rear right side of the house. Interestingly, this house was home to several varied types of animals at the time. Like attracts like in realms connecting the living and the dead.

Lights! Cameras! Cravings!

Above: STREET SIGN, 1ST NIGHT: As Hazel and I neared the front of the house to go in, I felt I needed to photograph the street sign as there was a darkness pervading the area of the sign, the bush, and the porch area directly behind it.

Right: BUNNY, 1ST NIGHT: Inside, we found nothing amiss at the window area and Ike sound asleep on the couch! I noticed the animals seemed disturbed and I got on the floor to get a picture of the bunny. Notice the dark black energy that completely blots out a portion of his ear but was not visible to the naked eye as I took the shot.

When Secrets Come to Life

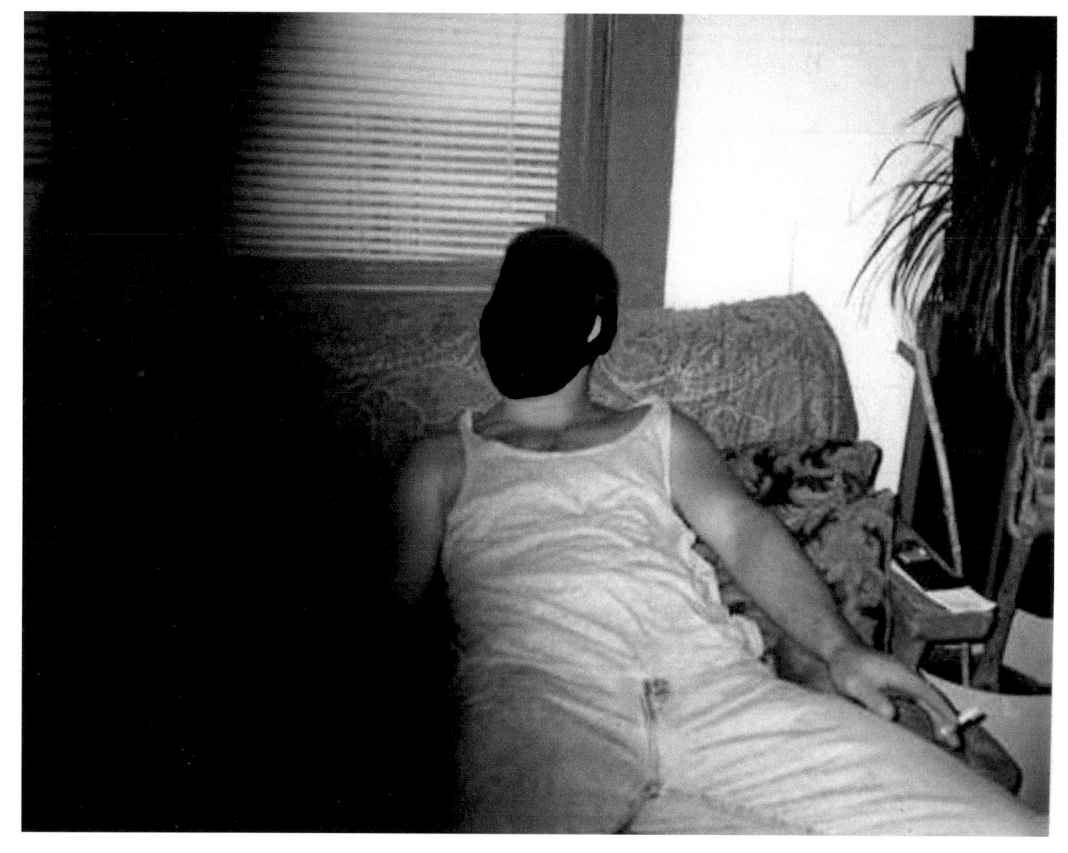

PORCH, 1ST NIGHT: Saying my goodbyes, Hazel and Ike (who was intoxicated) started arguing as they sat together on the front porch. Feeling awkward, the only thing I could think of doing was take a picture and quickly leave. Imagine my surprise when seeing the dark energy now completely obliterating Hazel's image.

gotten photographic evidence of an other-worldly nature. They decided to include a highly recommended psychic (also from CT) as part of the episode. They allotted me two days (during a typical nor'easter blizzard) to unearth any facts and info on the house and former owners. I was mad at myself for not researching this prior, as I should have, from the usual sources—town hall tax assessor's office, the former owners and occupants, etc. I came up empty-handed and no reports of anything unusual were found. However, many of the life-long neighbors recalled the house being a sort of "drug-den that attracted bad elements" for as far back as they could remember. This would explain the needles and syringes that had been found throughout the cabinets and closets when the family first moved in.

Content with my efforts, they scheduled a two-day "shoot" for the following week. With no time to think about petty worries like what I would wear or what I should say on camera, I was propelled into gathering photos and more importantly negatives so that *Sightings* could have them analyzed by experts at the Brooks Institute of Photography in Santa Barbara, California.

Lights! Cameras! Cravings!

The day arrived to meet the director and video and sound crew to start filming at the location. Brian Ochrym of Mirage Productions did all the video recording, Adam was the sound technician, and Kathryn Douglas the producer. After a few preliminaries and errands, we were ready to begin. I did my best to film them filming us during the day. Ike went missing, but Hazel was interviewed regarding her impression of the haunting and she frankly answered that she knew something otherworldly was causing the events in her home. The rain outside was not conducive to re-enacting the shadow ghost incident (there goes the hairdo, I thought on take #4), but filming continued inside and out, with the crew canvassing the layout of the structure.

Joyce St. Germaine, the psychic *Sightings* had chosen, arrived around 5:30 p.m., accompanied by her friend, Paul, who serves as a channel on occasion for spirits to communicate through while he is under hypnosis. I found them both to be immediately likable and knowledgeable regarding the paranormal. Joyce was interviewed on camera and proceeded to mentally scan the house and property. She was extremely accurate in pinpointing hotspots in the home and touched on some of the occurrences that had been going on. At one point when she was harnessing a mass of "stagnant energy" emanating from a doorway in the dining room, I reached my hand into the area of the invisible mass and felt my fingers tingle and become very warm. She stated that many animals in spirit form were congregating at this site in a sort of protective manner, and Hazel confirmed that all sorts of living wild animals seem to find their way to her property.

NIGHT OF THE TV SHOW *SIGHTINGS* FILMING: Hazel with baby as the camera crew began set-up of equipment. Joyce St. Germaine can be seen in the background.

Joyce related where she felt "portals" or openings to other realms could be found, and of where certain reconstruction of property lines had occurred. She claimed she felt the phone lines were often manipulated by spirit energies, and just then two brand-new $40 bulbs used by the cameraman exploded, two candles on separate candelabras flickered and blew out, and the phone rang twice—both times with a strange tone on the other end! My camera rewound itself causing me to think that I could open the case to load new film, when in fact it really hadn't rewound itself and the film, being exposed, was ruined. All of this happened at once and without any apparent, explainable reason. The huge energy surge was a great distraction! It succeeded momentarily in diverting our attention from the subject matter being discussed. Getting replacement bulbs of that type would take some time as well.

I thought this would be a good opportunity to scout around for Ike and give him a last chance to be a part of the show, if he wanted to—no pressure. Nearing the communal hallway shared by the other tenants, I smelled the strong odor of marijuana coming up from the basement doorway. "Ike? You down there?" He didn't answer so I just shut the door and went looking for room spray, air freshener, perfume, anything that might mask the smell.

I did the best with whatever I found and got back to the group. "No luck," I shrugged my shoulders and glanced at Hazel, and then over to the doorway downstairs. She understood just from my look and helped me to redirect them away from the basement area.

Armed only with flashlights, we proceeded to the attic. While taking snapshots up here alone earlier in the day, I saw a single blue orb up near the ceiling in one of the rooms and noticed a weird, machine-like humming noise. I stood frozen listening intently only to find it was a cat purring, and I assumed one of Hazel's had followed me upstairs. I looked everywhere, and no cat or other animal could be found. Ms. St. Germaine pointed out changes in construction of the attic that she had mentioned earlier on camera and went into a light trance. She claimed there were many beings who gathered at this location in human and animal form, particularly a long-haired cat. The animals, she said, "were all of a benevolent nature and felt comfortable here," whereas the earthbound spirits were a different sort altogether. They preyed upon the couple's weaknesses and Ike's penchant towards drugs and alcohol, allowing them to feed off the negative energy given off and fueled by the human hosts.

The psychic informed Hazel (Ike was still AWOL and not participating) that she would clear and close the portals metaphysically, which would help to prevent so many entities entering and using the home as a sort of wayward waystation, but that the couple should seek not only spiritual assistance but couples counseling, AA meetings, etc.

The day was growing long, and the crew felt that they had enough footage and left the premises shortly after Ms. St. Germaine and her friend. By the time I arrived home, unwound, and tended to household business, it was very late, and I crawled into bed. In no time at all, the alarm went off, and it was time to get back up and get myself camera-ready (as well as the house) as the crew were expected at 10:00 a.m. to finish filming at my home.

They arrived for the equipment set up, and this time it was my living room that was besieged by cameras, sound booms, and lighting stands. The director moved through my house looking for the perfect background spot for my on-camera interview and decided the best setting would be in a chair, diagonal to the fireplace. They moved furniture and rearranged pictures to make my space more "homey." It was only after all was said and done, and they'd packed up and left, that I'd discover the damage; I also learned that the tape they used to stick the cables to the carpet (so no one tripped) left a sticky residue that I never really got to come up or stop getting stuck to. This was my brand-new carpet, dammit! They strung their lighting on my hanging plants, totally frying and scorching bunches of leaves that could have caused a fire! I learned about the many aspects of creating a TV segment and how it takes several hours of filming just for one minute of usable footage!

Sitting where I was positioned, with lights and cameras staring at me, I felt like everything I said and did was seemingly magnified, making it difficult for me to focus on all the "profound" things I had wanted to communicate through this medium (pun intended). Nervously tapping my fingers, the sound guy told me he was picking up the noise. Also, my bracelet was too jangly and had to be removed. I squirmed around like a kid at church, and Kathryn reiterated the fact that everything could be edited, and I was appreciative for that. I answered questions of all kinds; one question, in particular, stands out: "Donna, what would you say to the people who think you're crazy or just making this stuff up?" Without skipping a beat or any hesitation, I replied, "There's always going to be skeptics, and whether they believe me or not I really don't care. I have more skeptics calling for my services than believers! It's amazing how freaked out they are when supernatural things happen to them, literally shattering their reality!" Forty minutes later and the interview was over, which had been the hardest part for me. I realized why I had felt so self-conscious—I'm usually the one asking the questions and conducting the interviews.

We went for a quick bite to eat and proceeded to various local haunted locations where I previously had gathered mounting piles of psychic photographs. It was 20 degrees outside, and after a short while, I was shivering with cold. We worked outside for over two hours and thirty minutes in a cemetery (which always happens to be colder than anywhere else!) and finally it was a wrap.

We exchanged hugs and business cards, and I led them to the highway entrance, where we beeped mutual goodbyes. I got home, thrilled with having such an experience, but exhausted, nonetheless. I was thankful it was over. I immediately changed into sweats, ordered Chinese take-out for dinner, and took the phone off the hook.

4
WHEN THE LIVING HAUNT THE DEAD

Or *High School Hellcats** and other Juvenile Delinquents

2002, West Haven, CT

Let me tell you a story. It happened a while ago but could still occur anytime, anywhere, when people get stupid or to take a leaf from a 1950s cheesy teen drama.

The whole thing started one night when a woman called me unrelentingly insistent that I should come to her house immediately.

"There is a ghost scaring my kids!" "Okay," I was scrounging around my desk for some paper and a pencil. "What can you tell me about them?" "They're dead." "Yeah, no shit," I thought but didn't say out loud. "Okay, that usually comes with being a ghost." "And she's Jewish." "She? Okay, that's different. How do you know that?"

The woman took a deep breath before rushing on with her story.

"The woman who appeared to my daughter was wearing a Star of David." Apparently, one of the lady's three daughters was awakened out of sound sleep to find a woman in a pink dress that looked like something out of the 1940s standing at the side of her bed. Around her neck, she wore the Star of David and was surrounded by a shimmering light, like a blue aura. "Said it looked like the sparklers we used to get for 4th of July," the mother said. We think they're coming in from the cemetery next door."

I agreed this could be something that needed to be pursued, that Cosmic would be out in a day or two to start an investigation. But it wasn't until later we found out that the woman had left out a few important details that weren't discovered until the team had arrived there a few nights later. The house had these weird looking pock marks in the siding next to the front door light, the lawn hadn't seen a lawnmower in a few weeks, and the house needed a bit of picking up. Ok, a lot of tidying up, like from a cleaning crew with a roll off dumpster.

After setting up the camera and recorders for the initial interview, the twin fifteen-year-old daughters who'd seen the lady appear didn't want to be filmed and left the house, proclaiming that they had better things to do. The mom was not too forthcoming with our questions, and the father was more than cranky, so he shut himself up in the bedroom, refusing to be interviewed by any of us or even say hello.

OK, there's a little hostility there, it's nothing that a little time and patience couldn't improve. It's common, most don't like to air their dirty laundry in front of strangers, or at least not until the really scary stuff starts to happen. Hopefully the dead folks next door would be a trifle friendlier. During the walk through of the house, the team felt a strong energy coming from the open doorway to the attic, which was just off the daughters' bedrooms. Energy that was like a thick heavy cloud of—the words weren't coming, but there was someone who could put action instead of words to that feeling.

"C'mere Amy, what do you feel?" Amy Brown was a talented girl with a sense for all things ghostly. And she had not stood in the doorway for more than ten seconds before she bolted down the stairs and flung herself out the front door, tossing up her lunch, supper, and any future plans for a snack on the way home. "There is just so much anger in that house." Even when she stepped back on to the porch, Amy made a beeline back out to dry-heave next to her car. "Those pock marks, next to the porch light," she gasped, "are bullet holes. My boyfriend is a cop, he's shown me enough crime scene pictures so I know what they look like." Well, somebody isn't very popular in the neighborhood. That's when I decided it was time to contact Dan, the psychic I'd ask to come in from time to time to help with the "clean outs." After the usual pleasantries (you know the ones: how's the weather, the kids, the dog, the cat?) we got down to business and dug into what was going on. In the following week, I mailed a package containing notes of Amy's psychic impressions and dreams along with the videotaped interview of the family to Dan and his wife, Ellie.

Amy had made very thorough notes as she had picked up on the hostilities that family was manifesting and collecting in nasty little pockets from the cellar to the attic, compounded with the piles of laundry, gobs of dog hair, cigarette butts, and broken glass that made things worse. The tape, unfortunately, fell short and silent. Something had gone wrong when I copied the tape, and the audio had been lost. Sigh, a not uncommon hazard for not only video tape, but photographs as well, when negative energy wants to distort sound and images to delay its removal. But the tape wasn't a total washout. Dan and Ellie watched the silent images, studying the body language of the people involved. These were some unhappy, desperate, but secretive folks, with something none of these people wanted to talk about.

But now the question was, how does a haunting involving Jews differ from one involving Christians? The trouble was no one in Cosmic had any idea. Christian, Santeria, and Wicca, Cosmic had a good bead on. The Hispanic, Portuguese, and Italian cultures were covered in abundance, but we were very light on Jewish. Enter the AOL Jewish Chatroom (as I keep saying: this took place a while ago). And so, I made the plunge, "please God, don't let them think I'm a total nut!"

With honesty being the best policy, and since there was no other way to explain why I was there, I plunged in with the truth. The following is what happened next:

Cosmic: "Hi, I'm a paranormal investigator and am going to a house where it appears to be haunted by a female Jewish ghost."

[Nothing. Not that I blame them.]

Cosmic: "Honest. And I need help. I know how to clear a house using the Christian, Wiccan and Santeria traditions, but I don't know anything about the Jewish way."

[There was scattered talk, some to me, some to each other and then an IM (instant message) popped up on my screen.]

Marfy: "Are you serious?"
Cosmic: "As a heart attack."
Marfy: "Aren't you afraid of looking into this stuff?"
Cosmic: "Yes. But I'm more afraid if I don't do anything."
Marfy: "Ok, here's an email address of this guy I know who can help you. In the subject line put this: Emergency: Marfy sent me. He'll know you're OK."
Cosmic: "Thank you so much!!"

So, that's what I did. I wrote to him with details of the case, my name, address, telephone number, and the Cosmic Society website address. And then hoped against hope that he didn't think this was totally "out there." Not only did Elliot Sands not think this was totally wacky, but two days after having sent that email, he called, and I was able to give the lowdown on what was going on. I also gave him Dan's phone number for him to call and discuss how to relate to a Jewish ghost.

Somewhere during that two-hour conversation with Dan, my friend had commented that his great-grandmother on his mom's side was a Jewish lady from Krakow, Poland, to which Elliot said, with a touch a humor in his voice, "Shalom Brother, you just solved the problem of who's going to read the prayers if you need to." According to Jewish law, a person is still considered to be Jewish if there is a Jewish ancestor on their mother's side of the family. No matter how far back.

Interesting fact: the Torah forbids communicating with the dead, which could be why there might be so few reports of Jewish hauntings (apart from Greenwich Village in NYC which seems to hold some attraction for the semite supernatural). There is also the belief that when the body dies, the spirit goes with it.

But there is one very famous Jewish ghost story, and you'll find it in the Torah or the Bible's Old Testament: First Samuel 28:1-20, King Saul and the Witch of Endor. Saul, who rid his kingdom of all witches, necromancers, and magicians, was worried about his army's upcoming battle with the Philistines. He didn't have his trusted advisor, the prophet Samuel, who had died unexpectedly. Secretly, Saul went to consult the Witch of Endor. After some convincing, she summoned the spirit of the prophet Samuel, who complained about being disturbed but also predicted Saul's downfall, which of course happened the next day.

So, continuing with Jewish 101: G-d has seventy-two names or aspects (G-d is spelled without the vowel as a sign of respect not bad spelling) covering one's head to keep one's soul safe as it's believed to be seated in the head. Also bring iron, like bolts, washers, or screws. When asked why, Elliot said it's believed that iron can't be crossed by the dead, which is why most old cemeteries have wrought iron gates or fences somewhere on the property. Better safe than sorry. "We believe in judgment after death, depending on your misdeeds in life. This governs the amount of time you spend in Gehinnom. A place that's not like Hell but more of a waiting room-which is kind of some people's idea of Hell. After you do penance you can leave for Olam Hebah aka Heaven."

When the Living Haunt the Dead

Elliot also left Dan with this thought: "if it turns into something bigger, I've got the phone number of a Hasidic order in New Haven. The Hassid are the ones who deal with hauntings and possessions, think of them like the Jesuits of Judaism. And if it's really bad, I've got the fax number of a Kabbalist in France." Day-am, that man came prepared.

When we came back the following Saturday, Cosmic was greeted to a typical suburban neighborhood of lawn mowers on full weekend roar, laundry hanging on the line, and a plethora of above-ground swimming pools teeming with small children all seemingly intent on drowning each other. In the middle of this sea of suburbia was the subject of our attention. That simple, green, two-story home, in need of a touch of paint here and there, but looking so normal (except for the bullet holes in the siding).

"Are you sure this is the right place?" Dan asked. "Yeah, this is it." I replied. "Guess they ran the lawnmower a little. Oh look, there's the rest of the team." Waiting on the front porch was Susan, Amy, and two new members, one of whom introduced himself as Randy. The family this time was a whole lot more cooperative for the follow-up visit. Even the father was there and a lot more attentive, even halfway hospitable. Something had obviously happened in the meantime. "The lady appeared at the side of my bed again!" The first twin explained. "She gave me the same kinda' look that my math teacher gives every day … er, sometimes … when I forget my homework … sometimes." The other twin chimed in too. "The lady said, 'Don't worry, Randy will help you.' But I don't even know a Randy!" Dan glanced over to the newest Cosmic member with fresh interest.

"Randy will help you," I wrote down on the steno pad I was using to make notes during the interview. The lady ghost didn't sound threatening. Nothing she did was menacing, dangerous, or harmful. Of course, that's when that creepy feeling came up the back of my neck; creepy, but again, nothing like I'd felt in some of the more infested places we've been to.

My head felt electric when my hair got lifted. (© 2002 A. Haley for Cosmic Society)

I was sitting on the floor trying to coax the family dog out of its crate when I could feel a chunk of hair on the back of my head rise and start to twist at the bottom. Kind of like how hair reacts to static electricity. I heard the click of a camera go off to the side and thought about what the results of that picture might be when it came out. Okay, someone is trying to get my attention.

I decided it was time for a little fresh air (combined with a cigarette) and to see what our ghost lady wanted. I'd wandered through the house, back to the mud room, and out onto the rear deck. The backyard was a happy jumble of toys, a swing set, and a fairly new above-ground swimming pool. Standing back about 300 feet from the house was a stand of weeds, bushes, and trees. Finding a faint path through the tangle, I picked my way through to find a chain-link fence, a twisted mass of vines, and a large blue tarp. Peeking over the fence, I saw the tarp was holding in a pile of junk that was trying to plug a rather large hole in the failing barrier. Since the clients had, in addition to their small poodle, a rather large pit bull, this little arrangement made perfect sense.

"Well, Marfy," I said out loud, "Score a big one for you." Guess this is what the ghost lady wanted me to see. Prior to leaving for our client's home, Elliot had called one last time with some feelings Marfy had on the case. She'd gotten the impression of a large hole in a fence separating the client's home from the cemetery. Apparently, the dead were slipping through the hole, and with the aid of electrical energy from the pool water and some kind of invitation, which Marfy wasn't clear on, the dead were able to gain entry to the home.

Coming back through the thicket, I met Dan, Ellie, and the rest of Cosmic coming out the back door, having left Susan to finish her part of the operation—a sage smudge and prayers that would hopefully clear the house. Now that she has our attention, let's go into the cemetery to find our ghost lady.

The cemetery was divided up into various sections by different religious societies, synagogues, and organizations. The problem now was not only to pick the right section, but the correct tombstone; one that was positioned just right for the spirit to make an appearance. Elliot had explained that Jewish ghosts do things in a series of left turns, so everything had to be set up in such a way for the ghost to turn left, leave their grave, head straight through the fence, over the pool, and into the house. Next, to appear to whomever and then have a window on the left to leave through, then make another series of only left turns to get back to the cemetery and the grave.

This made perfect sense regarding what the girls saw; that the ghost always came in through the back window, would make her appearance known on the left side of the bed, then turn left heading through the window between the beds to the sidewalk in front of the house and then turn left onto the side street with a final left back into the graveyard.

The dead were rather forthcoming that day. A little put out at first maybe, but they warmed up after a few introductions and seemed more than up for visitors after a couple of quarters and trinkets were left as offerings. Strolling about with Ellie, leaving coins, steel nuts, and washers in our wake, we went from section to section looking for some clue as to the mysterious lady with the Star of David necklace until Dan wandered into view in his stocking feet, shoes in hand. "Come on," he called out. "I think I've found who we're looking for." "Stone in your shoe?" I asked. "No," he replied. "Just a request. You know, energy comes in from the ground through the feet. Besides, this is holy ground, consecrated … any cemetery is really, it's a respectful thing."

When the Living Haunt the Dead

The first shot taken at the Jewish cemetery shows nothing abnormal.

Seconds later, an intense bright yellowish white energy was visible, but only to the camera.

The next moment we were all standing in front of a plain gray marble monument. Like the others, it bore both name and dates in both Hebrew and English. "It's her," Dan said quietly. "She's the one. The grave is in the correct position to make the series of left turns." "Ruth Gordon," I read. "Huh. What's your problem with the folks next door, Ruthie?"

"You mean other than those charming 'young ladies' we met pushing over tombstones, doing the Ouija board, drinking beer, shooting out the cemetery sign and having sex with their boyfriends in here?" Dan asked with a touch of sarcasm in his voice. "I wouldn't have the slightest idea why Ruth would be upset." Our ghost had just dropped a major dime on those two girls.

Which now really made sense as Elliot had said that a cemetery in Jewish tradition was a holy place, where one went to pray for the dead. Custom dictated that use of this sacred space for pleasure, fun, or frivolous behavior was forbidden. Modest dress, including head coverings for both men and women, was considered respectful. No eating or drinking on the grounds were allowed. I wondered what the consequences for their "other" activities might be. Oy Vay!

So, out of their disrespect, the girls created the invitation Marfy had picked up on. "Okay," I asked, "So now what?" Dan looked back in the direction of our client's house, rubbing his bearded chin and then over to Ruth Gordon's grave. "Give me some time to think on it and what she wants done." Then he strolled off with Randy to discuss what they felt should come next. Not too much later we all met up at the cemetery gates. "Think we're ready to finish up at the house?" I asked.

"I think so," Dan said absently. "We're just about ready to dish out a little tough love." Back in the living room, we set the family down to explain the situation:

> OK, what I'm seeing here is not only a clash in this family but a clash in cultures. We have you, Dad, retreating from any confrontations and leaving all the disciplining to Mom, which always results in arguing with your daughters, creating negative energy. Susan has taken steps to alleviate any lingering energy, but you'll have to do your part to not bring

Angry-looking gray and white energy in the Jewish cemetery during the day. Just before this photo was taken, the investigator saw a bunch of kids running from the graveyard, a tipped-over headstone, and empty liquor bottles. (© 2002 D. Burrows for Cosmic Society)

it back. The time is NOW, before a tragedy happens to restructure the rules in this house. The fact that these girls and their friends are carrying and using firearms, doing drugs and underage drinking needs to be addressed TODAY, not to mention the other things they've been up to. Your daughters have been going out into the cemetery to "play."

He gave them a stern look, "Which brought in the lady from the cemetery."

"But who's Randy?" The one daughter whined. "I still don't know any Randy!" Here Dan smiled. "Yes, you do." And with that, he pointed to the newest member of Cosmic. "He's going to be your point of contact on any further problems you might have. Randy is going to leave his phone number and if the lady shows up again, give him a call." Apparently, Ruth knew we would be coming, knew she had to get someone's attention somehow, and since Randy is highly psychic, sensitive to the spirit world, and local, she had tuned in on him.

The Rx for the situation: cut back on the fighting, stay out of the cemetery, and buy a box of Kosher salt for the backyard area in front of the hole in the fence. "To keep the folks from over there," Dan pointed over to the cemetery, "From coming through and into your house. Pour a line of salt in front of the blue tarp, asking the folks to respect the living as you, the living, respect the dead." Yet again he gave a hard look at the girls who this time had the good graces to cringe a little. "This should take care of the situation until we can get a hold of the cemetery association to come and fix the fence."

Years have passed and all's been quiet. The clients had never contacted Randy, so no news is usually good news. As far as we know, the cemetery fence was fixed, and after two messages to the local rabbi (the first for notification, the second for directions to the hole), nothing more was heard. Of Ruth Gordon there was this one night, a few weeks after we'd come back, when I was online with Marfy. She'd wanted to hear how everything had turned out. When I got to the part about Ruth Gordon, Marfy quickly typed, "did the people say what the ghost looked like?" Moments after I typed in the description, this came back:

Marfy: I had a teacher named Ruth Gordon at the Jewish High School I went to back in the mid-70s, who was from New Haven, CT. The kids gave her such a hard time, that in the middle of the school year she left. I always felt kind of bad about it. When did she pass away?
  Cosmic: 1978.
Marfy: That would have been about the right time, she was an older lady... Do you think?
  Cosmic: Could be…
Marfy: I think I'll be lighting an extra candle next Shabbos.
  Cosmic: Me too.

That Friday morning, in front of the Congregational Beth Israel synagogue holding a small white candle burning in memory of a very special lady, Dan, Ellie, and I were there. "Thank you, Ruth," as Dan began to recite a small part of the Ahava Rabbah or morning prayer for Ruth Gordon: "With great love, you have loved us, Lord, our God; with a great and abundant compassion have you had compassion upon us."

**High School Hellcats* is a 1953 American International Pictures production. It is an exploitation film about female juvenile delinquents.

5
IN AND OUT OF OWLSBURY

Otherwise Known as ... You Know ... That Place We're Not Supposed to Talk About

WHENEVER TO 1999

First, let me start by saying, you know where I'm talking about and don't bother going there. It's been closed since the fall of 1999 (thanks *Blair Witch Project*) and shows no sign of opening back up. Last I knew there was a $200 fine for trespassing; I suspect it's gone up a bit since then. Now that's a curse, and boy do I have a few choice curse words for that.

Okay then, let's start at the beginning. The Dudley's. Yes, there I said it. The Dudleytown, CT, Dudleys were not related to the Dudleys of England; not Sir Edmond Dudley, who was tax collector extraordinaire for King Henry VIII, nor Mr. Robert Dudley, who tried to woo Queen Elizabeth I and did a bunch of other really interesting stuff. No, sorry guys, no relation, which was the basis of so many starts to the Dudleytown story. No, not related, but yes, it's far more interesting than that.

Once upon a time there was a niche between two mountains and one hill in the northwest part of what became known as Connecticut. Pale settlers came from across the waves, chopped down the trees, built houses from them, and attempted to create a new Zion. But the land had other ideas, and being old and patient, it waited. Time passed and the original settlers left or passed away while others came to take their place. And so it went, the comings and goings until now, in the twenty-first century, it stands quiet save for the owls' and the wind's lonesome call.

We're going to start with the fact there was no one there, except for the animals. If ever there was a desert, in the meaning of absolutely no mark of humanity at all, then that was Litchfield County and Dudleytown in particular. So how do we know this? Because it was recorded in a book that was published in 1852 by the Connecticut Historical Society called *History of the Indians in Connecticut* by John W. DeForest. Yes, I do have a copy:

Above left: A sketch of what Dudleytown may have looked like in its early stages.

Above right: A warning literally etched in stone at one of the entranceways to what used to be the settlements, now just crumbling cellar hole rocks and boulders.

Above left: The Claw! These tree roots show no sign of letting go of their rock. Just like those who perpetuate the incorrect history of the ancestral roots of the Connecticut Dudley family.

Above right: No trespassing signs posted at one of three entrances.

> The whole country now known as Litchfield County together with the northern part of Fairfield and the western part of Hartford counties presented an uninhabited wilderness. The birds built their nest in its forests, without being disturbed by the smoke of a single wigwam; and the wild beasts who made it their home, were startled by no fires save those of a transient war-party or a wandering hunter.
>
> *History of the Indians in Connecticut*, p. 51

Now the book goes on to say that if there were ever any tribes living there, they got chased out in the early part of the seventeenth century when Iroquois war parties would come through on their way to raid the coastal tribes. So now that you have an idea no one was living there, where did all the traumatic stories come from? And how and where does the infamous "curse" come in? The first mention of it came from the book *They Found a Way* by Iveagh Hunt Sterry and William H. Garrigus in 1938. They, of course, thought there was a royal connection, like everyone else (even me) for a long time, until technology and genealogy made it possible to track the Dudley family back to, well, not the high-society Dudleys, though that narrative still continues. I'm guessing folks just don't want to let the truth get in the way of a good story. But to be fair, I could find no records to substantiate the name "Owlsbury" which is thought to be the area's original moniker—and yet (tsk, tsk) I'm guilty of using it in the chapter title.

I wrestled with so many questions: who were these Dudleys? Who were the rest of the people who came to live there? Why is it so haunted? Let's start at the beginning, Guilford, Connecticut, the year of 1639.

William and Jane Dudley, along with their infant son, William II, landed in Guilford, Connecticut, and shortly thereafter moved north roughly 20 miles to Saybrook. They remained there for three generations until Gideon Dudley decided to move further northwest up the Housatonic River Valley. His name first appears in the annals of Cornwall in 1747 as "witness" on a land deed. The following year, records state Gideon bought a tract of land from Thomas Griffis that lay between two mountains: Bald and Coltsfoot, along with what became later known as Dudleytown Hill.

The idea behind the purchase was sound: the property seemed to be blessed with usable water from the underground springs, the land appeared good for farming and the elevation would avoid the annual problems of Spring flooding when the Housatonic would ritually overflow its banks.

Thinking of joining Gideon's good fortune, other members of the Dudley family shortly arrived in the area as well. Initially, it was his brothers, Abial and Barzillai, along with his cousin, Martin Dudley. Soon, others from Saybrook and nearby hamlets followed, and an unofficial town sprung up on that little niche between the mountains, named after the founding family. It would have no town hall, no church, and no official cemetery, but it became known on local maps as Dudleytown.

To improve their chances of good fortune, records would later reveal that the Dudleys were rather industrious schemers. In a short time, Barzillai became the official surveyor of land for the town of Cornwall, and just prior to obtaining this position, the Dudleys purchased 90 acres of forest on Coltsfoot Mountain. Soon thereafter, the same land was resurveyed by Barzillai and resold as 100 acres.

An orb on the right at the waterfall.

    The problems with this part of Northwestern Connecticut soon made themselves apparent. The topsoil was bone thin, rocky, and poor for farming. Nonetheless, they managed to grow some crops of wheat and rye. The wheat they sold at market, but the rye the farmers kept and ate themselves. The abundance of water and the surrounding mountains which first appeared as an asset soon became a liability in that the dampness and shade accelerated the rate of mold and spoilage. The mold that grows on rye bread is called ergot. Ergot has the same chemical composition as LSD-25, so hallucinations would occur when eaten in small amounts, death in large. So, was it any wonder tales soon circulated of Dudleytown's people seeing, along with other things, "St. Elmo's Fire" before they went totally mad?

    The winter weather would add additional problems, the temperatures would be at least 10–20 degrees colder in the mountains than down below in Cornwall. Children and the elderly froze to death in their own beds because it was too cold to venture out for food and fuel. One can imagine the sound of the wind and wolves, howling their hunger through that white frozen wasteland, while perhaps something else, much darker and ancient, howled its craving for the human soul, biding its time. Ill luck seems to now shadow the Dudley family.

    Gideon seemed the hardest struck of all. His wife passed away, soon to be followed into the grave by his two small children. By 1768, he had sold off the major portion of his land and then lost the rest to creditors for reneging on his debts. After that, Gideon Dudley seemed to disappear into the mists of time. Barzillai marched off with Company 10 of Lyman's 3rd Regiment to fight in the French Wars in 1757 and never marched back. Martin intermarried with Sarah Dudley, his first cousin, on June 21, 1763, had two children, then disappeared also.

    By 1771, the Dudleys would be gone, save for Abial. Poor Abial was sixty-three, senile, and a public charge (a form of eighteenth-century welfare) where he'd be auctioned off every year to be cared for by the lowest bidder. Whatever lands he had owned were confiscated by the town. It was General Herman Swift and several others

When Secrets Come to Life

A house doesn't have to still be standing to be haunted as this orb at an old stone cellar hole might indicate.

A big orb at night.

who oversaw the land that was sold at public auction to reimburse those who paid the pittance for Abial's care.

There was also the unsolved murder/sudden death (depending on which story you want to go with) of one Gershom Hollister. In 1792, he went to lend a hand, some sweat, and muscle to a neighbor's barn raising. It's never been clear whether he fell or was pushed from the top of the roof to his death. Again, we're left only with speculations; of course, the worse the speculation, the better the story. The tales of folks dying of lightning strikes, while shocking (pun intended), of course, are not unbelievable—it happens!

Now bad things happen everywhere, but why here and not somewhere else? Maybe because of where Dudleytown sits in the triangle of ley lines that form over the Litchfield Hills. Energy begets energy, either positive or negative, and this place seems to draw in the negative, specifically—especially when you have sixty years of ghost stories, tall tales, and people doing insanely stupid stuff to draw it in! Drinkin' and druggin' teens and adults stumbling around day or night, daredevils who act like jerks even without being inebriated, and you get the idea of the troubles that can invariably ensue. They're the "just plain dumb" and annoying elements, except when they accidentally (or not?) set fires and cost the town and its rescue squads valuable resources. Somebody's got to fly the search and rescue helicopters, go find these idiots on foot, and extricate them out of the woods. Ambulances are called and fire brigades must somehow douse the flames.

Now envision all the "Blessed Wanna-Be" witches, warlocks, and sorcerers, who know not what they do, but do it anyway—like playing Ouija out in the woods in the dark until something supernatural happens, giving the land opportunity to take its revenge, when, running for their lives, they happen to fall off a cliff or trip and break a couple bones. These folks embody the second form of idiocy to plague the forest. Worse yet and dangerously more serious are the groups that do know the "high magick" and are all too well versed in the rituals and sacrificial ceremonies. They know these practices create magnetic fields, which draw in certain frequencies, and they know how to align that energy with the naturally occurring properties of the land.

It's hard not to have compassion for the homeowners who live up that way, who've had to endure sixty years of imbeciles stumbling around their property lines at any given hour, especially on Halloween. Heaven only knows what they were up to and the damage that was caused.

Okay, now we have ley lines. We have ergot (nothing like taking a trip and never leaving the farm). We have hard work and too many hard times. Never being able to make a go of things, even with the trees being cut down for charcoal and farming. The land was just not as fertile as it should be. Even with the large deposits of iron pyrite, it was just not enough to support and hold the people there. But what those pyrite deposits did do, when combined with running water, was create a magnetic field. These fields, known to seasoned ghost hunters, can affect cameras, video equipment, and some sensitive people. So, are we saying everything that happened up in Dudleytown can be explained away scientifically? No, not everything. Some of it, yes. But ley lines, naturally occurring electromagnetic fields, real witchcraft, and the energy of fear can create doorways or portals which can attract and allow "things" to come through, especially on Halloween.

Speaking of Halloween, let's look at that one day when the astral veil is thinnest, and people are at their stupidest, particularly in a place like Dudleytown. It is here that we, believe it or not, actually got a homeowner to talk to us. This is what she said:

When Secrets Come to Life

Examining the literal remains of what appeared to be an animal sacrifice.

Blue mist at night in Dudleytown.

My husband and I had left the city years ago to escape the crowds, pollution and crazies to come up here. I paid a lot of money to buy enough land to get some privacy and what I thought would be peace and quiet. No, I never saw anything ghostly and in fact I don't believe in them or the so-called "Curse of Dudleytown." The only curse I'm finding are all the weirdos who feel they have the right to come up here in the middle of the night to stumble around the woods, build bonfires and leave their garbage behind. Do you know how much trash I take out of this place? On any given day, I could walk the trails and take out three big garbage bags full of beer and soda cans, paper, half-eaten food and a lot of other disgusting things. Is this fair? To me … the forest … the other people of the Dark Entry Forest Association, who spent their hard-earned money to get away from the city for clean air and quiet? It seems I left one kind of weirdo behind in the city … only to be bombarded by even more of them out here in the middle of nowhere. Halloween is always the worst. I spent most of last night chasing kids out of the woods. I mean, the last group was out there at three o'clock in the morning! Do these kids' parents know where they are? If you're going to tell anyone about Dudleytown, you tell them my side of the story too.

While listening to the woman talk, I was half tempted to send her over to Dan and let him show her the photos. The spirit's face in the tree would be a real convincer, once she looked at the uncanny likeness from it and the man showing it to her! I opened my mouth to call him over but luckily stopped just in time as I realized that it wasn't the best idea. The woman wouldn't want to believe them, and besides, we could leave; she'd still had to live there. I just nodded and gave my word of honor to tell her side of the story.

At least the trespassers left their empty beer case outside the perimeter at this entrance.

In the tree bark on the upper left appears a man's head with sunglasses, hair coiffed, and mustache. Weirdly (and I mean super weirdly) it looks just like Dan, the photographer!

And as you can see, I did. And nothing scary happened that day. Nothing showed up in the pictures we took, it was as if anything that was up there took a powder for the day. Not very scary, huh? For the record (and the record books), let's pick another day with Dan and Ellie taking up the story from here.

* * * * *

Hi folks, Ellie at the computer and here comes the scary part. Imagine, if you will, deep snow, sub-zero temperatures, cabin fever, and boredom beyond mental reckoning. Let's not turn back the clock over 200 years, but merely a weekend in February 1999. That was a great year for a lot of things, getting ready for Y2K, the Euro became a type of currency, the artist formerly known as "Prince" made a great song, and we had snow. Not as much as some years, but respectable enough to be a pain in the neck. The blowing snow left drifts that kept us stranded in the house, with the car buried where the city plows had interred it. Bored, Dan and I stood idly at the window watching the snowfall. "Can you imagine what it's like in Dudleytown right now?" he said, writing the name on the frost-covered window.

"Huh-uh," I replied, automatically wiping out the letters he put up. "Everything that ever died up there because of the cold and snow is probably out there wailing among the trees."

There were accounts of children and old people dying in their beds when the drifts were too high, and no one could venture out for wood and food. But even if they got out and brought back provisions, it wasn't always in time to save their loved ones. Slow death from cold and starvation usually claimed them first. "My, aren't we cheerful." Dan replied, walking away from the window and back to the TV show he'd been watching. "But when the weather clears up, wouldn't you want to go up and see what it's like?"

With the information gleaned from town hall records, library, and all the other sources, I started to write about Dudleytown past and present. Considering most newspaper and magazine articles rehashed the same old crap, I was on a different approach. Not only would I try to lose the old myths and unsubstantiated stories but hunt for new ones; from new avenues of research, our own experiences, and those of the people we'd met along the way. It would be a week before traveling was possible, so by Friday we were ready to call Donna, when the wall phone in the kitchen rang (told you this was 1999), and speak of the devil, look who was on the other end of the line.

"You going to Dudleytown this weekend?" were the first words that she said without an ounce of "hi, how you been?"

"We'd thought about it," I replied, taking a moment to walk out into the living room (thank goodness for 20-foot phone cords). "It's Donna," I mouthed to Dan as I sat down on the couch, scratching the chin of the cat who had jumped into my lap. "Did you wanna go and meet up at the bookstore in West Cornwall?"

"Sure, I've borrowed a friend's VCR camcorder," she said excitedly. "If the ghosts show up for still shots, there's no reason why they shouldn't show up on video tape." Donna hesitated, "I'll make sure everything's in working order and grab a small fortune's worth of extra battery packs. Oh, and more importantly, ask for the good Lord's blessin'." she said in a terrible attempt at a southern accent. Turning serious, she said, "I did make a promise to return it in one piece." Considering how many cameras we'd all lost to that site, I assumed Donna's friend had no idea what D-Town was all about or why she wanted to borrow it in the first place.

Saturday dawned as bright as last Monday had been stormy. We left early that morning, with a lot to do and only a few good hours of daylight to do it in. Nearly 90 miles and a couple of pit stops later, we crossed over the covered bridge into West Cornwall and parked in front of the bookstore. Since Donna hadn't arrived yet, Dan and I walked across the road to the old house that stood grandly on the hillside, seeming not as foreboding as it had last fall, but almost fresh and new in the crisp chill of the last days of winter. At that time, it stood abandoned with one hell of a cold spot, orbs and images of someone standing in a window.

A group of investigators at the Mission School with cloudy-looking energy.

As Dan and I were down the hill taking a few slots of the exterior, Donna came up from behind us. "Hey guys, what took you so long?" she asked while looking at an invisible wristwatch. She held up the camcorder to start filming. "Anything interesting?" Dan asked her as we got back to the cars to head on to the next destination. "Not really, I only just started recording you guys," she said with a smirk. "Aww, ouch!" Dan said, feigning pain in his heart with his hand over his chest and bending at the waist, "You know you love us," he choked. "Yes, I do, but don't go having a heart attack, okay?" We all laughed and acknowledged it didn't matter how long a span between us, our camaraderie was as if no time had passed at all. We had a spontaneous hug and ventured out together.

A short time later, we stood at the gates of the Cornwall Cemetery. As with the house in West Cornwall, this too appeared clean and almost picturesque. Sunlight glittered off the snows of the rolling Connecticut hills, where the dead slept peacefully under a patchwork quilt of white, shadow, and stone. As Donna, Dan, and I wandered among the monuments, the crunch of snowpack underfoot and the huffing of our breath were the only sounds in the still frosty air. Every now and again, wind gusts would create little whirling dervishes of the snow piles and send them, sparkling and magical, seemingly straight for us.

Being that daylight was dictating our movements, we had to leave and hurry on to Dudleytown. The Cornwall Highway Dept. had done a good job with its sand and salt, because Bald Mountain Road was cleaned down to the concrete and sanded to the point where a lot of it had blown off the road and was accumulating in dirty little drifts on either side. Driving up, Dan once again looked at the house that we'd seen being built over the summer. It was now a completely snug, upwardly mobile dream home of some city couple who'd escaped the wilds of the city for the "wilds" of Connecticut. Little did they realize how wild it could get just a half mile further up the road.

After parking the car where the pavement now ended in the snow drifts, we got out, and Donna took out the camcorder and started taping. She checked the battery pack and the extra in the camera bag before pulling on her snow boots and locking her car. Dan seemed to be hooked earlier than usual (he once described Dudleytown as "calling to him") and went on down the snowy path seemingly with wings on his heels. Donna and I wandered in at a more leisurely pace. The woods were too beautiful to hurry through that day—or so it seemed.

Halfway down the path and still no sign of Dan, I started to get a little worried. It's never good to be wandering around up here by yourself. (Famous last words, as that summer I did go up there alone when an early morning server failure at work meant I was at loose ends for the day. I didn't tell Dan until months later, as I would've never heard the end of it. Story for another day.) There was a side path before you got to the first cellar hole that sucked. Really, it did. An energy draining vortex which drew you in and sucked you dry. And standing there up to his knees in a snow drift was Dan. Staring blankly down the path.

Wading over into the drift, "Dan?" I asked softly, "are you okay?" When he didn't answer and his gaze remained glassy, "DAN!"

"WHAT?!" That made him jump and land butt first into the snow. What he said next would not pass the editorial staff, so let's just say it wasn't "Merry Christmas."

"What happened?" Donna had been videotaping the scenery and had stopped to help me pull Dan out of the snow.

In and Out of Owlsbury

Right: A beautiful shot that almost makes Dudleytown seem clean and innocent. Beware though! Just when you start thinking that is when "it" strikes!

Below: I never saw this flying orb until the photos got developed. It appears to be close to the camera.

"I'd gone down to the vortex area almost not knowing how I got there," he said, brushing the snow off his back side. "Or caring why, except all of a sudden, I came to a screeching halt in front of the path leading to the vortex. Looking about, I suddenly saw her. About 30 feet away in the snow, a woman was standing among the trees as if waiting for me." Now he shivered. "She was tall and thin, and wore a long black dress with a yellow shawl wrapped about her shoulders. Her complexion was an unhealthy thickly pasty decaying yellow, which made her eyes appear as deep black hollows..."

Now I was shivering, but it wasn't from the cold. Dan continued:

> She was so real I raised my hand and waved at her. That's when she started moving toward me. Not walking, no, she floated, like you see ghosts do in the movies, across the snow. She was still far enough away for me to look through the camera's viewfinder and sure enough, I could see she was still there, so I kept taking pictures. Then her body faded to gray, the yellow shawl seemed to get sucked up into her face.... But ... her ... head ... kept ... coming!

Donna and I were now taking quick looks around, making sure wherever this spirit was, it wasn't coming back for a second run.

"Floating through the trees at me," Dan was now holding the small camera tight in his fist and against his chest. "She still showed up through the viewfinder and I kept on clicking pictures. Then the next thing I knew that ugly pasty face zoomed right at me, and I was staring, inches away with only the camera between us ... into those great ... black ... deep ... eyes! Ugh" He shuddered and looked around furtively, "Then I felt her..." He struggled to find the words, "Pass right through me! The next thing I know, you guys are standing there."

"Did you know the battery compartment on your camera was open?" Donna reached over and slid a finger into the compartment. "There are no batteries in there. Looks like they're gone, and I don't see them anywhere. You'd think we'd see where they fell." Dan hugged the camera tighter. "We gotta get outta here. Gotta go somewhere to get this all down while I can still keep the image fresh." "You don't have to ask me twice!" Donna said, and turning around, we trudged back up the path, away from the vortex, which I was not sad to see behind us.

Our first stop was to drop the film at a One-Hour Photo Booth in Canaan, CT, as none of us could wait to see if there'd be any type of results. Next (and as usual) we were all starving. We decided on the Collins Diner there in town, a little Silk City diner that maintained its ambiance and good pricing (again this was 1999), having eaten there a few times after tramping through the woods. After ordering, Dan took a page out of a small notebook he kept in his pocket and started drawing. After a few moments, he stopped and turned the page toward Donna and me. "This is what I saw, her body just faded away, but her head kept coming."

In the days that followed, he drew her constantly. Adding color, details, and things I did not want to know.

Above left: First photo in the "Woman in the Yellow Shawl" series. According to Dan, she would have been standing about where the curve in the path is. Note the upper and side edges of the picture are beginning to blur. Looking at this one always makes me dizzy! Also, strange that he could see her as a human figure, but the camera failed to capture her image as described.

Above right: In the second photo, a grayish mist has collected more energy, seen at the upper area.

In the third shot, we see the top right of the picture is now solid black, but a large, round, yellow mass follows behind.

When Secrets Come to Life

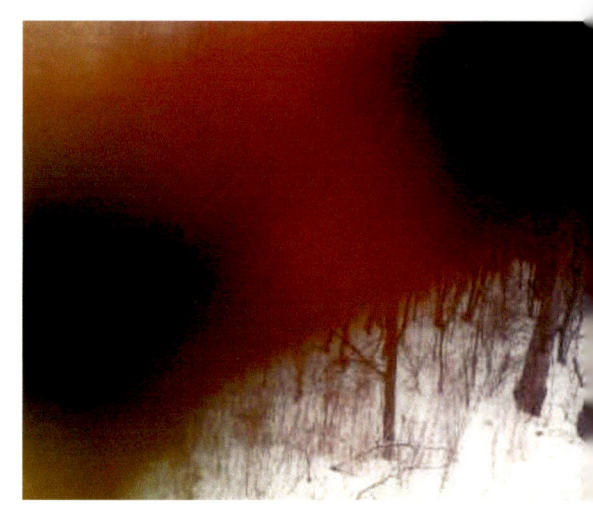

Above left: One of the best sets of a documented haunting encounter. The yellow face (or what's left of it) started speeding towards the investigator. What sort of intelligence was behind those eyes?

Above right: It got closer … and closer.

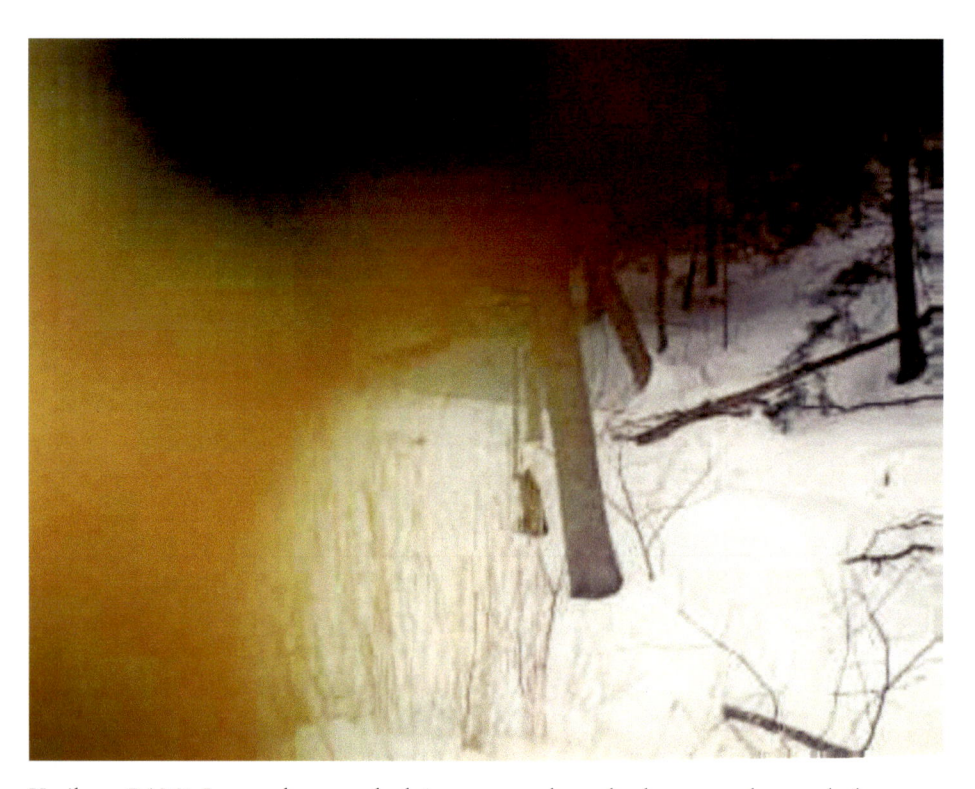

Until … BAM! It somehow pushed its energy through the researcher and then was completely gone. Or so we hoped!

In and Out of Owlsbury

Right: The actual binder page of sketches he drew less than an hour after the incident. In the drawings, Dan depicts what he saw coming towards him during the ordeal through the camera's viewfinder—although what he saw and what the device picked up vary slightly, the idea matches identically to the photos! Which, when drawn, had not yet been developed.

Below left: This is how the "Woman in the Yellow Shawl" looked when Dan first noticed her. Thinking she was a real person, he raised his hand to wave, only to then realize, with a sinking stomach, how out of place and improperly dressed she was for the weather.

Below right: Ready for take-off! In this sketch, we see the lady about to start gliding over the snow. At this point she is still a full-figured apparition.

When Secrets Come to Life

One of Dan's drawings shows when the lady's head detached from her disintegrating body and started flying right at him. I'm still fascinated as to what the camera picked up and what was seen visually.

* * * * *

Okay, it's me, Donna, again. When summer came around, Cosmic Society went up to scout around old Owlsbury with a few different groups of like-minded researchers. We weren't there to cause trouble, start fires, and drink ourselves into another reality. No, we tried to leave the place better than we found it. We brought extra garbage bags and picked up any trash we came across regardless of who left it there. And after a few excursions of being there in the dark, we made it a rule to never stay past dusk. It was important to keep track of where you were and about how long it would take to retreat; the dark closed in fast, really fast, when you weren't paying attention. More than once, it happened, and it was easy to lose your bearings. Luckily, we always had at least one tracker or weekend survivalist with us, who led us back. Others have not been as lucky. With these last few jaunts, "things" had shown up in our pictures like never before. Did the spirits know this may be their last chance for a close-up with Cosmic? Since time doesn't matter in the spirit world, did they know their images would be shown in a book almost thirty years later? I wonder how they feel about the internet.

* * * * *

Hey there, Ellie again. I just wanted to add this, maybe my "alone" story couldn't wait for another day. That June 7, I arrived to work at the insurance company. I was your basic wage slave/claims rep and was greeted at the door by one of the IT guys. "What's up Henry?" Then we noticed how quiet everything was, no phones ringing, no clack of computer keys, and a noticeable lack of the smell of coffee left too long on the burner. "Where is everybody?"

"Both servers went down, Worf and Picard went belly up," Henry explained. Yeah, our IT department was full of Trekkies (was really tempted to say, "It's dead, Jim, dead!") "Home office in Virginia has no idea when they will be back up. So instead of everyone sitting around doing nothing, they told us to send people home. Take it as a vacation day or make up the time during the rest of the week." Great, what a wonderful way to start the week.

But then, maybe it was a great way to start the week. Dan and I hadn't gone up to Dudleytown that weekend; it was my sister's birthday and there was no way I was going to miss that, or ever hear the end of it if I had. But maybe today would be the day to go and not bring Dan with me. I just wanted to see the place by myself. I'm brave, have gone into haunted houses, and been part of clearings—successful clearings. So, this was my chance to prove to everyone (i.e. myself) that I could do anything on my own.

Stopped off at the bank, got a quick $20 out the ATM, and headed to Connecticut. It would be a fast trip, nothing that would take a lot of time, and I would be home toot sweet with no one the wiser. The back roads through the Berkshires of Massachusetts went by in a blur and didn't take long to pass by Lime Rock Connecticut, West Cornwall, and then to Cornwall Bridge. Up Bald Mountain Road where it dead-ended at the path leading down into Dudleytown. Cut the engine and stepped out the car, only to realize maybe I really didn't think this through well enough. A pencil skirt and heels were not the best thing to go hiking trails.

But I'm here, and, oh, what the he… heck. I said heck, not hell. I'll just have to be a little more careful than usual. With a quick protection prayer under my breath, I started down the trail. I had to pick my way, avoiding rocks that could trip or muddy spots that a 2-inch heel could sink into. Things were going okay, nobody around, just me and the woods, the blue sky—and the dark thing peeking out from behind a tree.

Uh oh, that's not good. I walked a little further in and started seeing that dark thing now getting a little closer and now behind a different tree! It was kind of shaped like a person, tall, but just a shadow. A couple of more steps and now it was really close, like 10 feet close. Still no features, just a shadow in the light of day with no human around to cast it. Okay, this is when I realized what a mistake I'd made, so I turned and ran. In those days, I was a gazelle in high heels. I dashed up the path, not daring to look back to see if the thing was behind me or reaching out to grab and drag me back! I made it to the car and dropped the keys. Good God what was I? Some dope out of a bad horror flick? You know, the girl who was gonna get gutted like a trout by Jason, Freddie, or Leatherface because she drops her car keys and fumbles with the lock. But I did get the key in finally, yanked open the car door, threw myself in, and slammed it shut. Safe! But, yes, I did look in the back seat just to make sure the black thing wasn't waiting to jump forward and grab me. Nope, not there.

Driving home I wondered if I should tell Dan what happened. That I went up without him, and what I saw in there. No, not today. Not in the mood for a lecture, to defend

When Secrets Come to Life

my actions, and get into a fight where he will go on and on about "how could I not tell him things," and I would come back with why he didn't confess to burning a hole in the couch cushion, putting it out with a beer and not telling me until six months later when I discovered it! Sorry, it still bugs the crap out of me. Yeah, I did tell him finally, and we did have that fight. And yeah, he was right; the couch ordeal was a totally different subject and it was nothing compared to going, alone, to one of the country's most haunted locations. OK! I got it! And I promised, never again!

* * * * *

Early fall came, and we went up one last time.

Above: I have no idea what it is, but this "red snake" energy has been photographed not only here at Dudleytown, but in other well-known haunted areas I've been to in Connecticut.

Opposite above: Ever feel like you're being watched? How about followed? On one visit to the forest, orbs seemed to be present around every one of us at different times and in different locations.

Opposite below: Yet another large orb trailing the researchers.

In and Out of Owlsbury

Lonesome orb on path.

You get an orb, and you get an orb! Everybody gets an orb!

Even a tree stump that looks like an old seafaring captain gets an orb!

Bringing the camera and the film to a professional developer with concerns that the device might have a defect causing a light leak, his keen eye pointed out that "Light leaks don't maneuver themselves in, around and behind objects. Also, what bent that tree into an arch?"

Taken at the exact same time with two photographers and two cameras. Nothing seems abnormal from this angle.

The second perspective is quite different, as is obvious in this photo.

Then came the closure. Apparently, *The Blair Witch Project* spawned a whole lot more idiots than anyone could have ever imagined. More people doing dumber and dumber things until the homeowners who lived up that way on Bald Mountain and Dark Entry Roads had enough. I did go to see the movie, though; the first half hour was just *so* Dudleytown, but it did a good job of exemplifying the naivety of most people who go stumbling around in the dark woods at night. Frankly I was done with that place. I didn't like how I felt after being there, even if it was a beautiful sunny day, birds were chirping, and nothing outwardly supernatural happened; there was always the feeling of "something's wrong." And it wasn't like I was helping anyone by being there.

In the blink of (an owl's) eye, the Dark Entry Forest Association closed it. They sent out a news release and made sure everyone knew about it and that the Connecticut State Police would be enforcing that ruling. After all these years, it was over. Dudleytown was now going to be silent forever, back to the way it was in the early seventeenth century. Silent, with nothing but the birds and animals passing through. Did that put the "Woman in the Yellow Shawl" back to sleep? Or the dark figure that peeked out from behind the trees? Did the multicolored mists and orbs dissipate into nothingness? We won't ever know unless what is up there comes down here, down the hill—to your town.

And if it does?

Cosmic Society logo. (© 1995 Donna Kent/Cosmic Society)